Programming in

Flex & YACC

Programming in
Flex & YACC

Vinu V Das

Tabor Press

ISBN: 978-1-997541-03-5

Table of Contents

Chapter 1: Introduction to Lexical Analysis and Parsing

Compiler construction is a fascinating field where theory meets practical application in the transformation of human-readable code into machine-executable instructions. At the heart of any compiler lie two critical processes: lexical analysis and parsing. These foundational phases work together to deconstruct, understand, and organize the raw source code into a structured format that can be further processed by subsequent stages of compilation. In this chapter, we provide a comprehensive introduction to lexical analysis and parsing, exploring their core concepts, methodologies, historical context, and importance in the overall compiler architecture. This chapter is designed to stand alone as a thorough primer, ensuring that readers gain a solid grounding in these subjects without overlapping with the more advanced topics discussed in later chapters.

1.1 The Role of Compiler Construction

Before delving into the specifics of lexical analysis and parsing, it is important to understand the broader context of compiler construction. A compiler is a complex software system that transforms code written in a high-level programming language into a lower-level representation, often machine code or an intermediate representation. The compiler is generally divided into several phases, each responsible for a specific aspect of the transformation process:

- **Lexical Analysis:** The process of converting a sequence of characters from the source code into a sequence of tokens.

- **Syntax Analysis (Parsing):** The process of analyzing the sequence of tokens to determine their grammatical structure and to build a parse tree or abstract syntax tree (AST).
- **Semantic Analysis:** The phase where meaning is attributed to the syntactic structures; this includes type checking, scope resolution, and other context-sensitive validations.
- **Intermediate Code Generation and Optimization:** The translation of the AST into an intermediate representation (IR) that can be optimized.
- **Code Generation:** The final phase that translates the optimized IR into target-specific machine code or another executable format.

Lexical analysis and parsing are the very first steps in this pipeline. They act as the gateway, taking the unstructured stream of characters and transforming it into a structured format that lays the foundation for all subsequent compilation stages. Their effectiveness directly impacts the accuracy and efficiency of the entire compiler.

1.2 What is Lexical Analysis?

Lexical analysis, often referred to as scanning, is the process of reading the raw source code and breaking it into meaningful sequences known as tokens. A token is a string with an assigned and thus identified meaning. Typical tokens include keywords (e.g., `if`, `while`, `return`), identifiers (names of variables, functions, etc.), literals (numeric values, string values), and symbols (operators, punctuation).

1.2.1 The Purpose of Lexical Analysis

The main objective of lexical analysis is to simplify the subsequent parsing stage. Rather than dealing with individual characters and raw input, the parser works with tokens that encapsulate the syntactic and semantic meaning of the input. This abstraction offers several benefits:

- **Simplification:** It reduces the complexity by categorizing raw input into a finite set of token types.
- **Error Detection:** Early errors, such as invalid characters or improperly formatted numbers, can be caught during the scanning phase.
- **Efficiency:** Processing tokens is significantly faster than processing a stream of individual characters, enabling more efficient analysis in later stages.

1.2.2 How Lexical Analysis Works

The process of lexical analysis is typically driven by a set of rules defined by regular expressions. These expressions describe the patterns that define valid tokens. The lexical analyzer scans the source code from left to right and applies these rules to group characters into tokens. Consider, for instance, the simple rule for identifying an integer literal:

- **Regular Expression for an Integer:** [0-9]+

This pattern matches one or more digits in a row. When the lexer encounters a sequence of digits, it classifies that sequence as a numeric token.

The lexical analyzer usually maintains additional information, such as line numbers and positions in the source code. This metadata is critical for error reporting, as it allows the compiler to pinpoint exactly where in the source code an error occurred.

1.2.3 Lexical Analysis Tools

Historically, tools like **FLEX** (Fast Lexical Analyzer Generator) have been used to automatically generate lexical analyzers from a set of regular expression rules. FLEX reads a specification file containing definitions, regular expressions, and associated actions, and produces a C source file that implements the lexical analyzer. This automation greatly simplifies the development of compilers by eliminating the need to write a lexer from scratch.

Modern alternatives and variations exist as well, but the core idea remains the same: define patterns for tokens and let a tool handle the transformation of raw text into tokens.

1.3 What is Parsing?

Parsing is the process that follows lexical analysis and involves analyzing the token sequence to determine its grammatical structure. This stage checks whether the token sequence conforms to the syntax of the language and constructs a data structure—typically a parse tree or an abstract syntax tree (AST)—that represents the syntactic structure of the program.

1.3.1 The Goal of Parsing

The primary goal of parsing is to translate the linear sequence of tokens into a hierarchical structure that captures the underlying grammatical rules of the language. This structure makes explicit the relationships between different parts of the program, such as which operators apply to which operands and how different language constructs are nested within one another.

1.3.2 The Parsing Process

Parsing involves several key steps:

- **Grammar Definition:** The parser relies on a formal grammar, usually a context-free grammar (CFG), that defines the syntax of the language. The grammar is composed of production rules that describe how tokens can be combined to form valid constructs.
- **Parse Tree Construction:** As the parser reads the tokens, it applies the production rules to build a parse tree. Each node in the parse tree represents a grammatical construct. The leaves of the tree are tokens, and the internal nodes represent combinations of tokens as defined by the grammar.

- **Error Detection:** During parsing, if the token sequence does not match any production rule, a syntax error is flagged. A robust parser will not only detect errors but also attempt to recover from them, allowing for multiple errors to be reported in a single pass.

1.3.3 Parsing Techniques

There are several parsing techniques, each with its own advantages and trade-offs. Two broad categories are:

- **Top-Down Parsing:** This approach starts from the start symbol of the grammar and works down to the leaves. Recursive-descent parsing is a common form of top-down parsing. While intuitive, it can struggle with left-recursive grammars and may require backtracking.
- **Bottom-Up Parsing:** This approach starts from the input tokens and works its way up to the start symbol by gradually reducing the token sequence to higher-level constructs. Tools like YACC (Yet Another Compiler Compiler) generate bottom-up parsers using techniques such as LR parsing. Bottom-up parsers are generally more powerful and can handle a broader class of grammars without backtracking.

1.4 The Relationship Between Lexical Analysis and Parsing

Lexical analysis and parsing are sequential phases in the compilation process, each with distinct responsibilities yet closely interrelated. Together, they transform a flat stream of characters into a structured representation of a program.

1.4.1 From Characters to Tokens

The lexer serves as the first filter, scanning raw characters and grouping them into tokens. These tokens are the building blocks for the parser. By converting characters to tokens, the lexer abstracts away the low-level details of the input and provides a cleaner, more manageable interface for the parser.

1.4.2 From Tokens to Parse Trees

Once the lexer has produced a token stream, the parser takes over. It uses the language's grammar to combine tokens into meaningful constructs, such as expressions, statements, and declarations. The resulting parse tree or AST is a hierarchical representation that reflects the syntactic structure of the source code. This tree is used in later phases for semantic analysis and code generation.

1.4.3 Error Propagation and Recovery

Both phases play a crucial role in error handling. Lexical analysis may catch invalid characters or malformed tokens, while parsing focuses on syntactic errors. Effective error recovery in the lexer can prevent the parser from receiving erroneous tokens, thereby reducing cascading errors in the subsequent phase. Similarly, robust parsing techniques can detect and recover from syntax errors, allowing the compiler to continue processing the input and report multiple issues.

1.5 Techniques and Algorithms in Lexical Analysis

The design and implementation of a lexical analyzer involve several sophisticated techniques that help ensure efficiency and accuracy. Here, we explore some of the key concepts and algorithms used in lexical analysis.

1.5.1 Regular Expressions and Finite Automata

At the core of lexical analysis is the concept of regular expressions. A regular expression defines a set of strings that match a particular pattern. These patterns are used to describe tokens. For example:

- **Identifier:** [a-zA-Z_][a-zA-Z0-9_]*
- **Number:** [0-9]+(¥.[0-9]+)?

Regular expressions are closely linked with finite automata—abstract machines that accept or reject strings based on state transitions. Lexical analyzers are often implemented as deterministic finite automata (DFAs) that efficiently recognize token patterns.

1.5.2 Lexer Generators: From Specification to Code

Tools like FLEX allow you to define regular expressions and associated actions in a specification file. The lexer generator then converts this specification into C code that implements the DFA. This automation not only speeds up development but also reduces the potential for human error in writing a lexer manually.

1.5.3 Handling Ambiguities in Lexical Analysis

Although regular expressions are powerful, they sometimes can match overlapping patterns. For instance, the string "if" might be interpreted as an identifier or a keyword, depending on the language rules. Lexical analyzers resolve such ambiguities by defining rule priorities—usually the rule that appears first in the specification takes precedence. This mechanism ensures that reserved keywords are correctly identified.

1.5.4 Optimization in Lexical Analysis

Efficient lexers are critical for the overall performance of the compiler. Techniques such as table-driven implementations, state minimization, and input buffering are used to optimize the DFA. These optimizations ensure that even very large source files can be processed quickly and with minimal overhead.

1.6 Techniques and Algorithms in Parsing

Parsing transforms a flat sequence of tokens into a structured representation. Various algorithms and techniques have been developed to handle the complexities of natural language syntax and programming language grammars.

1.6.1 Context-Free Grammars

At the heart of parsing is the concept of context-free grammars (CFGs). A CFG consists of a set of production rules that define how tokens can be combined to form valid syntactic structures. Each rule has a left-hand side (a non-terminal symbol) and a right-hand side (a sequence of terminal and/or non-terminal symbols). CFGs are powerful enough to describe most programming language constructs, including recursive patterns.

1.6.2 Parsing Algorithms: Top-Down vs. Bottom-Up

As discussed earlier, parsing algorithms can be broadly classified into top-down and bottom-up approaches.

- **Top-Down Parsing:** Recursive-descent parsing is a common top-down method. It is easy to implement and understand but can struggle with left-recursive grammars. Techniques such as left recursion elimination are used to adapt the grammar for top-down parsing.
- **Bottom-Up Parsing:** Bottom-up parsers, such as those generated by YACC, build the parse tree from the leaves upward. LR parsing is one of the most powerful bottom-up techniques. It handles a wider class of grammars and typically does not require backtracking, making it more efficient and robust.

1.6.3 Handling Ambiguity in Parsing

Ambiguity is inherent in many grammars. Ambiguous grammars can lead to multiple valid parse trees for the same input. Parser generators use various methods to resolve ambiguities:

- **Operator Precedence and Associativity Declarations:** These rules help the parser decide which operation to perform first in arithmetic expressions.
- **Grammar Refactoring:** The grammar can be rewritten to remove ambiguity, such as by separating expressions into different non-terminals for different operator precedence levels.
- **Conflict Resolution Mechanisms:** Modern parser generators provide ways to handle shift/reduce and reduce/reduce conflicts, ensuring that the chosen parse tree reflects the intended meaning of the input.

1.6.4 Error Handling and Recovery in Parsing

Error detection and recovery are critical components of parsing. A robust parser should not only identify syntax errors but also recover from them to continue processing the rest of the input. Techniques such as panic mode recovery, error productions, and context-sensitive error messages are used to achieve this goal. Effective error handling improves user experience by providing clear guidance on where and how to correct mistakes.

1.7 Historical Perspective and Evolution

The development of lexical analysis and parsing has a rich history that reflects the evolution of computer science and programming languages.

1.7.1 Early Developments

In the early days of computing, compilers were hand-written, and lexical analysis was often implemented using ad hoc methods. As programming languages grew more complex, the need for systematic and automated approaches became clear. This led to the development of formal grammars and the introduction of tools like Lex and YACC in the 1970s and 1980s. These tools provided a structured way to generate lexers and parsers, dramatically reducing the amount of manual coding required.

1.7.2 The Impact of Lex and YACC

Lex and YACC revolutionized compiler construction by automating the process of lexical and syntactic analysis. They introduced the concept of generating code from a formal specification, which not only improved reliability but also made the development process more accessible. Over the decades, these tools have been refined and extended, and they have inspired numerous modern alternatives.

1.7.3 Transition to Modern Tools

While Lex and YACC remain influential, modern computing demands have driven the development of new tools and techniques. The limitations of traditional tools—such as cryptic error messages, limited language support, and difficulties in integrating with modern programming environments—have led to the creation of more advanced parser generators and language workbenches. These modern alternatives build upon the principles established by Lex and YACC while addressing their shortcomings.

1.8 Modern Relevance of Lexical Analysis and Parsing

Even as new tools emerge, the fundamental concepts of lexical analysis and parsing remain as relevant as ever. Understanding these processes is crucial not only for compiler construction but also for a wide range of applications.

1.8.1 Applications Beyond Compilers

The techniques of lexical analysis and parsing are applied in many areas beyond traditional compilers:

- **Interpreters and Scripting Languages:** Many modern languages, such as Python and JavaScript, rely on interpreters that use lexical and syntactic analysis to execute code dynamically.
- **Data Processing and Transformation:** Tools that parse data formats like JSON, XML, and CSV use the same fundamental techniques to extract structured information from unstructured input.
- **Natural Language Processing (NLP):** While NLP often deals with more complex and ambiguous grammars, the principles of tokenization and parsing still apply.
- **Configuration File Processing:** Many applications require the parsing of configuration files to set up environments and parameters. Lexical analysis and parsing ensure that these files are read accurately and efficiently.

1.8.2 Educational Importance

Lexical analysis and parsing form the bedrock of many computer science curricula. They provide a practical introduction to formal language theory, automata, and the design of efficient algorithms. Through hands-on projects involving lexer and parser generators, students learn not only how to build compilers but also how to approach complex problem-solving tasks in a structured manner.

1.8.3 Continued Innovation

The field of language processing is continually evolving. Even as new tools and paradigms emerge, the core techniques of lexical analysis and parsing underpin many modern innovations. For example, incremental parsing, which enables real-time code analysis in modern IDEs, is built on the same principles as traditional parsing. Similarly, advancements in error recovery and debugging techniques continue to improve the robustness of compilers and interpreters.

Chapter 2: Understanding FLEX – A Lexical Analyzer Generator

Lexical analysis is the critical first step in transforming human-readable code into structured data that a compiler can work with. FLEX, which stands for Fast Lexical Analyzer Generator, is one of the pioneering tools that automates this process. In this chapter, we take an in-depth look at FLEX, exploring its internal workings, structure, and practical usage. We examine how FLEX converts a set of pattern rules into efficient, runnable C code and discuss advanced features, best practices, and techniques to optimize and debug lexical analyzers. This chapter is intended to stand alone as a complete guide to FLEX without repeating content from other parts of this book.

2.1 Introduction to FLEX

At its core, FLEX is a tool designed to automate the creation of lexical analyzers, commonly known as lexers or scanners. The primary purpose of a lexical analyzer is to read the raw input—a stream of characters—and partition it into tokens. These tokens, which represent syntactic units like keywords, operators, identifiers, and literals, are then passed on to the parser for further analysis.

FLEX revolutionized compiler construction by abstracting the intricate details of pattern matching and state management. Instead of manually writing complex code to identify tokens, developers can specify regular expressions and corresponding actions in a simple specification file. FLEX then processes this file to generate efficient C code that implements the lexical analyzer.

Key Objectives of FLEX

- **Automation:** FLEX automates the creation of lexers, reducing manual coding and potential human errors. It transforms high-level regular expressions into low-level, optimized C code.
- **Efficiency:** The generated lexers are designed to run quickly and efficiently, making FLEX ideal for processing large source files.
- **Simplicity and Flexibility:** The specification language used in FLEX is relatively simple, allowing developers to focus on the token patterns without worrying about the underlying implementation details.
- **Portability:** As FLEX generates standard C code, the resulting lexer can be compiled and run on any platform that supports C.

2.2 The Historical Evolution of FLEX

Understanding FLEX also means appreciating its history and the context in which it was developed. Early in the history of compiler construction, writing a lexical analyzer was a tedious and error-prone process. Pioneering tools like Lex (the predecessor of FLEX) emerged in the 1970s to address this challenge, providing a way to generate lexers automatically from formal specifications.

The Birth of Lex and Its Successors

The original Lex tool was developed at Bell Labs and laid the foundation for automated lexical analysis. As programming languages evolved and the demands on compilers increased, Lex became a staple in compiler design courses and industry projects. However, Lex had its limitations—particularly in terms of performance and portability. FLEX was introduced as an improved, faster, and more flexible alternative that built on Lex's ideas.

Improvements and Innovations

FLEX introduced several innovations:

- **Speed Enhancements:** FLEX is designed to be faster than its predecessor by optimizing the generated finite automata and reducing overhead in token recognition.
- **Memory Efficiency:** The generated code in FLEX is optimized to use memory efficiently, which is crucial when processing very large source files.
- **Extended Syntax:** FLEX supports additional features such as start conditions and more expressive pattern definitions, allowing for more sophisticated lexers.

These enhancements have made FLEX a popular choice for both academic research and industrial applications, maintaining its relevance even as newer tools have emerged.

2.3 The Role of Lexical Analysis in Compiler Design

Before diving deeper into FLEX itself, it is important to understand the role of lexical analysis within the broader context of compiler construction.

From Characters to Tokens

The input to a compiler is a stream of characters. For a human, these characters form a coherent program, but for a machine, the process of understanding code begins with breaking it into meaningful chunks. This is where lexical analysis comes in. The lexer reads the raw characters and groups them into tokens. Each token represents a syntactic element of the language, such as:

- **Keywords:** Reserved words like if, while, return, which have a special meaning.
- **Identifiers:** Names of variables, functions, and user-defined types.
- **Literals:** Numeric values, string literals, and other constant values.
- **Operators and Punctuation:** Symbols like +, -, *, /, (,), and ;.

By converting the character stream into tokens, the lexer reduces the complexity of the input, allowing the parser to work with a manageable and well-defined set of elements.

Error Detection at the Lexical Level

Lexical analysis is also the first opportunity for a compiler to detect errors in the source code. For instance, if the input contains an invalid character or an improperly formatted number, the lexer can flag these errors immediately. This early detection prevents the parser from attempting to process invalid input, reducing the chances of cascading errors.

The Interface Between Lexer and Parser

The output of the lexer is a stream of tokens, each often accompanied by additional information (semantic values, line numbers, column numbers). The parser uses this token stream to build a parse tree or abstract syntax tree (AST) that represents the hierarchical structure of the program. The clear separation of concerns between the lexer and parser is one of the reasons why tools like FLEX and YACC have been so successful.

2.4 Structure of a FLEX Specification

A FLEX specification is divided into three main sections, each separated by specific delimiters. Understanding the structure of these sections is crucial for effectively writing and maintaining a lexical analyzer.

2.4.1 The Definitions Section

The definitions section is the first part of a FLEX file, enclosed between %{ and %} markers. It typically contains:

- **C Code Inclusions:** This includes necessary header files, such as ⟨stdio.h⟩, ⟨stdlib.h⟩, and any project-specific headers like common.h or symtable.h. These headers provide declarations needed by the generated lexer.
- **Macro Definitions:** Developers can define macros for common patterns. For example, a macro for a digit can be defined as:

```
DIGIT   [0-9]
```

   Such definitions improve readability and maintainability, especially when the same pattern is used repeatedly.

- **Global Variables:** Variables that must be accessible throughout the generated code can also be declared here. For instance, you might declare a global variable to keep track of the current line number.

This section essentially sets up the environment in which the lexer will operate, ensuring that all necessary functions and macros are available.

2.4.2 The Rules Section

The rules section is the heart of the FLEX specification. It is where you define the regular expressions that match the tokens and specify the corresponding actions to take when those patterns are encountered.

Regular Expressions

Each rule in this section consists of a regular expression and an action, separated by whitespace. For example:

```
[0-9]+   { yylval = atoi(yytext); return NUMBER; }
```

This rule matches one or more digits, converts the matched text to an integer, assigns it to yylval (the semantic value), and returns the token type NUMBER.

Regular expressions in FLEX are based on standard pattern-matching syntax. They can be simple or complex, depending on the needs of your language. The flexibility of regular expressions allows for precise token matching and can even accommodate variations in input format.

Action Blocks

The action block is enclosed in curly braces { ... } and contains C code that executes whenever the rule is matched. Actions can perform a variety of tasks:

- **Token Conversion:** Converting a string to a numeric value or processing a string literal.
- **State Management:** Updating global variables, such as the line number or column position.
- **Returning Tokens:** Specifying which token to return to the parser.
- **Error Handling:** Handling unexpected characters or malformed tokens gracefully.

Each action block is crucial for bridging the gap between the raw input and the structured tokens that the parser will consume.

2.4.3 The User Code Section

The user code section appears at the end of a FLEX file, following the second delimiter %%. It contains C code that is copied verbatim into the generated source file. This section is typically used for:

- **Function Definitions:** Defining helper functions that support the lexical analysis process. For example, you might include a function for handling errors or a custom memory allocation routine.
- **Main Function:** In many FLEX specifications, a main() function is provided to drive the lexical analyzer. This function calls yyparse() (if integrated with YACC) or directly invokes the lexer.
- **Additional Declarations:** Any additional code that does not fit into the definitions or rules sections can be placed here.

This section ensures that the generated lexer is a complete, stand-alone C program that can be compiled and executed.

2.5 How FLEX Works: From Regular Expressions to Finite Automata

The power of FLEX lies in its ability to translate high-level regular expressions into efficient, executable C code. This transformation is achieved through the use of finite automata, specifically deterministic finite automata (DFAs).

2.5.1 Regular Expressions and Their Role

Regular expressions are formal descriptions of patterns in text. They serve as the blueprint for token definitions in a FLEX specification. When you write a regular expression in FLEX, you are essentially describing a set of strings that belong to a particular token class. For example:

- **Identifier Pattern:** `[a-zA-Z_][a-zA-Z0-9_]*` This pattern matches any sequence of characters that starts with a letter or underscore, followed by any combination of letters, digits, or underscores.
- **Floating-Point Number:** `[0-9]+¥.[0-9]+([eE][+-]?[0-9]+)?` This pattern describes the structure of a floating-point number, including an optional exponent.

These expressions are concise yet expressive, enabling the lexer to capture the full complexity of the language's lexical structure.

2.5.2 Constructing Finite Automata

Behind the scenes, FLEX converts each regular expression into a finite automaton—a mathematical model that represents the states and transitions necessary to recognize the pattern. The process involves several steps:

- **NFA Construction:** Initially, each regular expression is transformed into a nondeterministic finite automaton (NFA). NFAs are conceptually simple and directly represent the structure of the regular expression, including alternatives (using the union operation) and repetitions (using the Kleene star).
- **Subset Construction to DFA:** The NFA is then converted into a deterministic finite automaton (DFA) using the subset construction algorithm. A DFA has a unique transition for each input symbol from each state, making it more efficient for implementation.
- **Minimization:** In some cases, the DFA is further minimized to reduce the number of states, which improves the efficiency of the generated code.

The resulting DFA is implemented in the generated C code as a state machine that processes the input character by character. The state transitions dictate how tokens are recognized and when actions are executed.

2.5.3 Efficiency Considerations

The transformation from regular expressions to DFAs is a key factor in the efficiency of FLEX-generated lexers. DFAs allow for constant-time processing per character, which means that the lexer's performance is directly proportional to the length of the input. Furthermore, because DFAs do not require backtracking, they are well-suited for high-performance applications where large source files must be processed quickly.

FLEX also implements several optimizations:

- **Buffering:** The generated code uses input buffering to read large chunks of data at once, reducing the overhead of individual character reads.
- **State Table Optimization:** The DFA is represented as a state table in the generated C code, which is optimized for fast lookups.

These optimizations help ensure that the lexical analysis phase does not become a bottleneck in the compilation process.

2.6 Writing and Testing FLEX Specifications

Creating a robust FLEX specification requires careful planning, thorough testing, and attention to detail. This section outlines practical steps and best practices for writing, testing, and refining your FLEX specifications.

2.6.1 Best Practices for Writing FLEX Files

- **Clear Organization:** Organize your FLEX file into the three standard sections—definitions, rules, and user code. Group related rules together and use comments liberally to explain complex regular expressions or non-obvious actions.
- **Use Macros and Definitions:** Define common patterns as macros at the beginning of the file. For example, defining DIGIT and LETTER macros makes the patterns for identifiers and numbers more readable and easier to maintain.
- **Prioritize Rules:** Remember that FLEX matches the first rule that fits the input. Place rules for reserved keywords before those for identifiers to ensure that keywords are recognized correctly.
- **Modular Actions:** For complex actions, call helper functions instead of embedding large blocks of code directly within the rule. This makes the specification easier to read and debug.

2.6.2 Testing and Debugging Strategies

Testing your FLEX specification is crucial for ensuring that your lexer works correctly under all circumstances. Here are some effective strategies:

- **Unit Testing Individual Rules:** Create test cases for each rule. For instance, test the numeric literal rule with various inputs to ensure it correctly converts strings to numbers.
- **Automated Test Scripts:** Write scripts that run your lexer against a suite of input files and compare the output tokens with expected results. This regression testing helps catch errors introduced during modifications.
- **Verbose Debug Output:** During development, enable debug output by inserting print statements in action blocks. For example, printing the matched text and the token returned can help trace the lexer's behavior.
- **Interactive Testing:** Use small, interactive test programs that read input from the user and display the tokens generated by the lexer. This hands-on approach allows you to experiment with different inputs in real time.
- **Error Simulation:** Deliberately input malformed or unexpected data to see how the lexer handles errors. This testing can reveal weaknesses in your error handling and guide improvements.

2.6.3 Refining and Optimizing Your Specification

After initial testing, you may need to refine your FLEX specification to handle edge cases or improve performance.

- **Handling Ambiguous Patterns:** If two rules can match the same input, ensure that the intended rule is placed first. Adjust your regular expressions to be as specific as possible to avoid unintended matches.
- **Optimizing Regular Expressions:** Complex regular expressions can sometimes lead to performance issues. Use tools or online analyzers to review your regular expressions for potential inefficiencies, such as excessive backtracking.
- **Memory Management:** In your actions, pay careful attention to dynamic memory allocation. For example, when using functions like strdup(), ensure that the allocated memory is freed at the appropriate time.
- **Profiling Lexer Performance:** For large input files, profile the performance of the generated lexer. This can help you identify any bottlenecks in the state machine or in the handling of specific token types.

By iterating on your FLEX specification using these strategies, you can develop a lexer that is both robust and efficient, forming a solid foundation for the subsequent parsing phase.

2.7 Advanced Features and Customizations in FLEX

While the basics of FLEX are sufficient for many projects, advanced features and customizations can significantly enhance the power and flexibility of your lexical analyzer. This section explores several advanced techniques that can help you tackle more complex parsing challenges.

2.7.1 Start Conditions

Start conditions are an advanced feature in FLEX that allow the lexer to operate in different modes. This is especially useful when the lexical structure of the input changes in different contexts.

How Start Conditions Work

A start condition is essentially a state that modifies which rules are active at a given time. For example, consider a language where comments can appear within code. You might define a start condition for comment mode:

```
%x COMMENT
```

The %x directive declares an exclusive start condition named COMMENT. You can then specify rules that only apply when the lexer is in this state. To enter a comment, you might have a rule like:

```
"/*"   { BEGIN(COMMENT); }
```

And in COMMENT mode, you define rules for the comment body:

```
<COMMENT>{
  [^*]+   { /* Consume non-asterisk characters */ }
  "*" "/" { BEGIN(INITIAL); } // End of comment
  .       { /* Handle unexpected characters */ }
}
```

By using start conditions, you can manage complex lexical constructs that require different behaviors based on context.

2.7.2 Handling Multiple Token Types and Context-Sensitive Patterns

Modern programming languages often have context-sensitive lexical structures. For instance, the meaning of a token might change depending on whether it appears in a string, a comment, or code. FLEX allows you to write rules that take context into account, often using start conditions as described above.

Contextual Actions

For example, consider string literals. You might have different rules for the beginning, content, and end of a string:

```
\"       { BEGIN(STRING); return QUOTE; }
<STRING>{
  [^\\"]+  { /* Consume string content */ }
  "\\"     { /* Handle escape sequences */ }
  \"       { BEGIN(INITIAL); return QUOTE; }
}
```

This approach ensures that escape sequences are handled properly and that the lexer remains in the correct state throughout the string literal.

2.7.3 Custom Error Handling and Recovery

Error handling is critical in a lexer. FLEX allows you to define custom actions for unexpected input, providing detailed error messages and even attempting recovery.

Error Token and Reporting

You can define a rule to catch any character that does not match any other rule:

```
{
    fprintf(stderr, "Lexical error: unexpected character '%s' at line %d\n", yytext,
yylineno);
    /* Optionally, return a special error token or skip the character */
}
```

This rule ensures that any unexpected character is reported, giving you insight into potential issues in the input.

2.7.4 Performance Tuning and Memory Optimization

As discussed earlier, efficiency is paramount in lexical analysis. Beyond the inherent efficiency of DFAs, you can further optimize your FLEX specifications.

Buffering Strategies

FLEX uses internal buffers to minimize I/O operations. However, you can fine-tune buffer sizes using command-line options or directives in your specification. For example, adjusting the buffer size may be necessary for very large files.

Minimizing Memory Overhead

Memory allocation in action blocks should be handled with care. For instance, if you duplicate strings with strdup(), ensure that you have a corresponding mechanism to free them. Consider using memory pools or arenas if your lexer creates a large number of small objects.

2.7.5 Integrating FLEX with Other Tools

While FLEX is often used in conjunction with parser generators like YACC, it can also be integrated with other modern tools. For example, FLEX-generated lexers can serve as standalone components in larger software systems, including interpreters, data processors, and real-time applications. This modularity makes FLEX a versatile tool that adapts well to different development paradigms.

2.8 Case Studies: Real-World Applications of FLEX

To solidify our understanding of FLEX, we now examine several case studies that illustrate how FLEX is used in practical projects. These examples highlight the flexibility, efficiency, and adaptability of FLEX in different domains.

2.8.1 A Simple Calculator Lexer

One of the most common introductory projects for FLEX is a simple calculator. In this application, the lexer is responsible for recognizing numeric literals, arithmetic operators, and grouping symbols. The specification includes rules like:

```
[0-9]+    { yylval = atoi(yytext); return NUMBER; }
"+"       { return PLUS; }
"-"       { return MINUS; }
"*"       { return MULTIPLY; }
"/"       { return DIVIDE; }
"("       { return LPAREN; }
```

```
")"        { return RPAREN; }
```

This straightforward example demonstrates how FLEX abstracts away the low-level details of tokenization, allowing the developer to focus on the high-level design of the language.

2.8.2 Processing Configuration Files

Another common use case for FLEX is the processing of configuration files. Many applications require robust and efficient parsing of configuration data. A FLEX specification for a configuration file might include rules to handle key-value pairs, comments, and whitespace. For example:

```
"#".*       { /* Ignore comments */ }
[A-Za-z0-9_]+ { return IDENTIFIER; }
"="         { return ASSIGN; }
\"([^\\\"]|\\.)*\" { yylval = strdup(yytext); return STRING; }
[ \t\n]+    { /* Skip whitespace */ }
```

Such a lexer forms the basis for a configuration file parser that can be integrated into a larger application to load and validate settings.

2.8.3 Lexing a Domain-Specific Language (DSL)

Domain-specific languages (DSLs) are another area where FLEX shines. DSLs often have unique syntactic rules tailored to a specific problem domain. By defining custom token patterns, FLEX enables developers to quickly build lexers for DSLs without having to build the entire compiler infrastructure from scratch.

Consider a DSL for financial contracts. The lexer might include rules for currency symbols, dates, and identifiers unique to financial transactions. With a well-designed FLEX specification, the lexer can handle these specialized tokens efficiently, laying the groundwork for a parser that understands the semantics of financial contracts.

2.9 Best Practices and Future Directions in Lexical Analysis

As you gain experience with FLEX, several best practices emerge that can guide the development of robust lexical analyzers.

2.9.1 Writing Maintainable Specifications

- **Modularization:** Break down your FLEX specification into logical sections, use macros for repeated patterns, and organize rules by their purpose. This makes the specification easier to maintain and modify.
- **Documentation:** Comment your code extensively. Explain the purpose of complex regular expressions, the reasoning behind start conditions, and any non-obvious actions taken in the code.

- **Version Control:** Use version control systems to manage changes in your FLEX specifications. This allows you to track modifications, revert to previous versions if necessary, and collaborate effectively with other developers.

2.9.2 Optimizing for Performance and Reliability

- **Profiling:** Regularly profile your lexer with large input files to ensure that performance remains acceptable. Use tools such as gprof or custom instrumentation to identify bottlenecks.
- **Memory Management:** Pay careful attention to dynamic memory allocation within your action blocks. Ensure that all allocated memory is eventually freed, and consider using memory pools for frequently allocated small objects.
- **Error Handling:** Implement robust error reporting and recovery. A good lexer not only processes correct input efficiently but also handles unexpected input gracefully, providing useful error messages to aid in debugging.

2.9.3 Embracing Modern Developments

While FLEX remains a powerful tool, it is important to stay informed about modern developments in lexical analysis. Many contemporary tools build on the principles established by FLEX while offering enhanced features:

- **Integration with IDEs:** Modern development environments offer real-time lexical analysis and syntax highlighting, which can provide immediate feedback during code editing.
- **Cross-Language Support:** Tools that generate lexers for multiple target languages (such as ANTLR) are becoming more popular. While FLEX is tightly coupled with C, exploring alternatives might be beneficial for projects that require greater language flexibility.
- **Incremental Lexing:** For applications such as interactive development environments, incremental lexing—updating only the affected parts of the input—can provide significant performance improvements.

2.9.4 Future Directions

The field of lexical analysis continues to evolve. Researchers and practitioners are exploring new algorithms, optimization techniques, and integration strategies to further enhance the efficiency and usability of lexers. Future directions may include:

- **Machine Learning for Lexical Prediction:** Integrating machine learning techniques to predict token boundaries or correct lexical errors automatically.
- **Advanced Error Recovery Mechanisms:** Developing more sophisticated error recovery methods that provide context-aware suggestions to users.
- **Cloud-Based Lexical Analysis:** Leveraging cloud computing resources to handle extremely large inputs or perform real-time analysis across distributed systems.
- **Hybrid Approaches:** Combining traditional DFA-based methods with modern probabilistic models to improve both speed and accuracy in ambiguous or noisy inputs.

Chapter 3: Advanced Features of FLEX

Lexical analysis is a vital phase in the compilation process, and while the basic use of FLEX is straightforward, many advanced features make it a powerful tool for creating sophisticated lexers. In this chapter, we delve into FLEX's advanced capabilities, exploring how to handle more complex language constructs, optimize tokenization, and fine-tune error handling. We cover techniques for managing whitespace and comments, integrating symbol tables and keyword recognition, processing numeric constants and identifiers, employing start conditions for context-sensitive scanning, and implementing robust error handling. This chapter is designed to provide a deep understanding of FLEX's advanced features without overlapping with the more general topics discussed in earlier chapters.

3.1 Handling Whitespaces and Comments

One of the fundamental challenges in lexical analysis is dealing with parts of the source code that are not syntactically significant—whitespace and comments. Although these elements do not affect the semantics of a program, they must be handled correctly to ensure that the lexer produces the appropriate token stream for the parser.

3.1.1 Skipping Irrelevant Characters

In most programming languages, whitespace (spaces, tabs, and newlines) is used only to separate tokens. In FLEX, you can easily define rules to skip over whitespace so that it does not clutter the token stream. A typical rule looks like this:

```
[ \t\n\r]+    { /* Ignore whitespace */ }
```

This regular expression matches one or more whitespace characters. The associated action is empty, meaning that when this pattern is encountered, the lexer simply discards it and continues scanning. This rule must be placed appropriately—usually at the top of your rules section—to ensure that whitespace is not mistakenly processed as part of a token.

3.1.2 Handling Comments

Comments are another non-semantic element that should be skipped by the lexer. Languages differ in comment syntax; some use line comments (e.g., $//$ in C++ or Java), while others use block comments (e.g., $/* \ldots */$). FLEX allows you to define rules for each type.

Line Comments

For line comments, where the comment starts with a specific marker and continues until the end of the line, you can write a rule such as:

```
"//".*      { /* Ignore everything from '//' to the end of the line */ }
```

This rule uses the pattern $"//" . *$ to match a double-slash followed by any sequence of characters. The action is empty, so the entire comment is skipped.

Block Comments

Block comments, which begin with a marker like $/*$ and end with $*/$, require a bit more sophistication because they can span multiple lines. A simple rule might look like:

```
"/*"([^*]|\*+[^*/])*\*+"/"  { /* Discard block comment */ }
```

This pattern matches a starting delimiter $/*$, followed by any number of characters that are not the end delimiter, and finally the closing delimiter $*/$. However, because block comments can be nested or may appear in complex contexts, many developers prefer using start conditions (discussed later in Section 3.4) for more robust handling.

Advanced Comment Handling

Sometimes, you might need to process comments rather than ignore them. For instance, some tools extract documentation from specially formatted comments. In such cases, the action block associated with a comment rule might store the comment in a buffer or pass it to a separate documentation processor.

Example for documentation comments:

```
"/*!"([^*]|\*+[^*/])*\*+"/" {
    /* Extract and process documentation comment */
    process_doc_comment(yytext);
}
```

Here, comments starting with /∗! are recognized as documentation comments, and the function process_doc_comment() handles them appropriately.

3.2 Symbol Tables and Keyword Recognition

In many programming languages, certain words have a special meaning—they are reserved as keywords, while others are treated as identifiers. Advanced lexical analysis often involves distinguishing between these two classes, sometimes by integrating a symbol table or a keyword lookup mechanism directly into the lexer.

3.2.1 The Role of Keyword Recognition

Keyword recognition is critical because keywords trigger specific parsing behavior. For example, in a language like C, words such as if, while, and return have fixed meanings, whereas other words represent user-defined identifiers. The lexer must be able to differentiate between these categories to pass the correct tokens to the parser.

3.2.2 Implementing Keyword Lookups

A common strategy in FLEX is to treat all words that match the pattern for an identifier and then check if the matched string is a reserved keyword. This is typically implemented by calling a lookup function in the action block.

Consider the following snippet:

```
[A-Za-z_][A-Za-z0-9_]* {
    int token = lookup_reserved(yytext);
    if (token == IDENTIFIER) {
        /* If not a keyword, process as identifier */
        yylval = strdup(yytext);
    }
    return token;
}
```

In this rule, the regular expression matches any valid identifier. The function lookup_reserved() is then called to determine if the identifier is a reserved keyword. If it is not, the lexer duplicates the string and assigns it to yylval, then returns the token type. The lookup_reserved() function typically searches a static table of keywords defined elsewhere in your code.

3.2.3 Using a Symbol Table

For languages with a rich set of identifiers or where additional processing is needed (such as type checking), integrating a symbol table in the lexical phase can be advantageous. A symbol table is a data structure that stores information about identifiers—such as their names, types, and scope information. While symbol tables are primarily used in semantic analysis, incorporating a preliminary symbol table lookup in the lexer can help optimize the parsing process.

A basic approach might involve:

- **Inserting Identifiers:** When a new identifier is encountered, it is inserted into the symbol table along with default attributes.
- **Keyword Precedence:** The symbol table lookup can also be used to override generic identifier rules with keyword-specific tokens.
- **Memory Management:** Efficiently managing memory for identifier strings by reusing allocated memory or implementing string interning.

For example:

```
[A-Za-z_][A-Za-z0-9_]* {
    int token = lookup_reserved(yytext);
    if (token == IDENTIFIER) {
        Symbol *sym = lookup_symbol(yytext);
        if (!sym) {
            sym = insert_symbol(yytext, DEFAULT_TYPE);
        }
        yylval = (int)sym;
    }
    return token;
}
```

Here, lookup_symbol () checks if the identifier already exists in the symbol table, and insert_symbol () adds it if not. This integration supports more advanced language features and helps the parser later during semantic analysis.

3.2.4 Handling Case Sensitivity and Localization

Different languages have different rules regarding case sensitivity. In some languages, keywords and identifiers are case-sensitive; in others, they are not. FLEX allows you to manipulate the input to handle these variations. For instance, you can use C library functions to convert input to lowercase before performing a keyword lookup:

```
[A-Za-z_][A-Za-z0-9_]* {
    char *word = strdup(yytext);
    for (char *p = word; *p; ++p) *p = tolower(*p);
    int token = lookup_reserved(word);
    free(word);
    if (token == IDENTIFIER) {
        yylval = strdup(yytext);
    }
    return token;
}
```

This approach ensures that the lexer correctly handles case-insensitive languages while preserving the original text for identifiers if needed.

3.3 Handling Numeric Constants and Identifiers

Lexers must be adept at recognizing different types of tokens, and numeric constants and identifiers are among the most common and varied.

3.3.1 Numeric Constants

Numeric constants can be integers, floating-point numbers, hexadecimal values, or even scientific notation numbers. Each of these requires a distinct regular expression to match the correct pattern.

Integer and Floating-Point Numbers

A simple rule for integer literals might be:

```
[0-9]+     { yylval = atoi(yytext); return NUMBER; }
```

For floating-point numbers, you might extend the rule:

```
[0-9]+\.[0-9]+([eE][+-]?[0-9]+)? {
    yylval = atof(yytext);
    return NUMBER;
}
```

These rules use standard C library functions like atoi() and atof() to convert the text to a numerical value, which is then stored in yylval.

Handling Different Bases

Languages often support numbers in different bases, such as hexadecimal (e.g., 0x1A3F) or octal (e.g., 0755). FLEX can accommodate these by defining separate rules:

```
0[xX][0-9a-fA-F]+ {
    yylval = (int)strtol(yytext, NULL, 16);
    return NUMBER;
}
0[0-7]* {
    yylval = (int)strtol(yytext, NULL, 8);
    return NUMBER;
}
```

Here, `strtol()` is used with the appropriate base to convert the matched string to an integer.

3.3.2 Identifiers

Identifiers typically represent variable names, function names, or other user-defined symbols. The pattern for identifiers is usually defined by a combination of letters, digits, and underscores. A common rule is:

```
[A-Za-z_][A-Za-z0-9_]* {
    int token = lookup_reserved(yytext);
    if (token == IDENTIFIER) {
        yylval = strdup(yytext);
    }
    return token;
}
```

This rule not only matches the identifier but also checks if it is a reserved keyword. If it is not, the identifier is duplicated and stored for later use.

3.3.3 Handling Identifiers with Special Characters

Some languages allow special characters in identifiers or support Unicode. FLEX supports extended character sets, though it may require careful configuration. For instance, you might define a rule that supports Unicode letters:

```
[\p{L}_][\p{L}\p{Nd}_]* {
    /* Process Unicode identifier */
    yylval = process_unicode_identifier(yytext);
    return IDENTIFIER;
}
```

This approach ensures that your lexer can handle internationalized source code.

3.3.4 Combining Numeric and Identifier Rules

In some cases, numeric constants and identifiers might appear similar (e.g., leading zeros in numbers can be confused with octal values). It is important to order your rules so that the most specific patterns are matched first. For example, if hexadecimal numbers are supported, the rule for hexadecimal literals should come before the generic integer rule to avoid ambiguity.

3.3.5 Testing Numeric and Identifier Handling

Given the complexity of numeric formats and identifier rules, thorough testing is essential. Develop test cases that cover:

- Simple integers and floating-point numbers.
- Numbers in different bases.
- Edge cases such as extremely large numbers or numbers with unusual formatting.
- Identifiers that may be confused with keywords.
- Unicode identifiers if supported.

Automated tests can run these cases through your lexer and verify that the correct tokens and semantic values are produced.

3.4 Using Start Conditions for Context-Sensitive Scanning

One of the most powerful advanced features in FLEX is the ability to use start conditions. Start conditions allow the lexer to operate in different modes or contexts, enabling more sophisticated and context-sensitive scanning.

3.4.1 Concept and Purpose of Start Conditions

Start conditions provide a mechanism for the lexer to change its set of active rules based on the context within the input. This is especially useful when the meaning of certain sequences changes depending on where they occur. For example, in many programming languages, the contents of a string literal or a comment block must be treated differently from normal code.

3.4.2 Declaring and Using Start Conditions

Start conditions are declared using the %x (exclusive) or %s (inclusive) directives. An exclusive start condition means that only rules with that condition are active, while an inclusive start condition allows both the start condition rules and the default rules to match.

Example: Handling Comments

Consider a language where block comments are delimited by $/*$ and $*/$. You might define a start condition for comment mode:

```
%x COMMENT
```

Then, you can write rules that only apply when the lexer is in the COMMENT state:

```
"/*"      { BEGIN(COMMENT); }
<COMMENT>{
   [^*]+   { /* Consume all non-asterisk characters */ }
   "*" "/" { BEGIN(INITIAL); }
      .       { /* Handle unexpected characters in comment */ }
}
```

Here, when the lexer encounters $/*$, it switches to the COMMENT start condition. Within this state, only the rules prefixed with ⟨COMMENT⟩ are active, ensuring that the content is treated appropriately until the closing delimiter is found.

Example: Handling String Literals

String literals often require special handling due to escape sequences and termination conditions. You can define a start condition for strings:

```
%x STRING
```

And then write rules for entering and exiting string mode:

```
\"       { BEGIN(STRING); return QUOTE; }
<STRING>{
   [^\\\"]+  { /* Process string content */ }
   "\\"     { /* Handle escape sequences */ }
   \"        { BEGIN(INITIAL); return QUOTE; }
}
```

This method allows you to isolate the processing of string content from normal code, ensuring that escape characters and delimiters are correctly interpreted.

3.4.3 Advantages of Start Conditions

Start conditions offer several advantages:

- **Contextual Flexibility:** They enable the lexer to adapt its behavior based on context, allowing for the handling of complex, context-sensitive constructs.
- **Modular Rule Organization:** By grouping rules according to their context, start conditions make the specification more organized and easier to maintain.
- **Enhanced Readability:** With start conditions, the intention behind each rule is clearer. Developers can easily see which rules apply in which contexts.

3.4.4 Advanced Use Cases

Beyond comments and strings, start conditions are useful in more advanced scenarios:

- **Embedded Languages:** In some languages, you might have embedded code from another language (e.g., SQL inside a host language). Start conditions allow you to switch between different lexical analyses.
- **Preprocessor Directives:** Languages with preprocessor directives can use start conditions to differentiate between code that should be processed normally and code that should be handled by the preprocessor.
- **Template Processing:** When parsing templated languages (like HTML with embedded JavaScript), start conditions enable the lexer to switch contexts seamlessly, processing each part according to its own rules.

3.4.5 Testing and Debugging Start Conditions

Testing start conditions requires careful attention:

- **Isolated Testing:** Test each start condition in isolation with relevant input. For instance, feed only comment blocks to ensure that the COMMENT state behaves as expected.
- **Boundary Conditions:** Verify that transitions between states occur correctly, such as entering and exiting string mode.
- **Mixed Content:** Test scenarios where different contexts are interleaved (e.g., code with embedded comments) to ensure that the lexer switches contexts accurately.

Start conditions, when used effectively, greatly enhance the expressiveness of your FLEX specification, allowing you to build lexers that can handle sophisticated language features with ease.

3.5 Error Handling in FLEX

No lexer is complete without robust error handling. Advanced error handling in FLEX ensures that your lexical analyzer can gracefully recover from unexpected input, provide meaningful diagnostic messages, and continue processing where possible.

3.5.1 Importance of Robust Error Handling

Errors in lexical analysis can arise from various sources:

- **Invalid Characters:** Characters that do not match any defined pattern.
- **Malformed Tokens:** Improperly formatted numeric constants or strings.
- **Context-Sensitive Errors:** For example, an unclosed string literal or comment block.

Robust error handling not only improves the user experience but also aids in debugging by pinpointing the exact location and nature of the problem.

3.5.2 Defining a Catch-All Rule

A common technique in FLEX is to define a catch-all rule that matches any character not handled by other rules. This rule can be used to generate error messages:

```
{
    fprintf(stderr, "Lexical error: unexpected character '%s' at line %d\n", yytext,
yylineno);
    /* Optionally, you can return an error token or simply ignore the character */
}
```

This rule ensures that no input goes unexamined. If a character does not match any valid pattern, the lexer reports it immediately.

3.5.3 Contextual Error Recovery

Advanced error handling often involves context-sensitive recovery strategies. Using start conditions can help manage errors that occur in specific contexts:

Unterminated String Literals: In string mode, if the closing quote is never encountered, you can define a rule to handle the end-of-file in the STRING state:

```
<STRING><<EOF>> {
    fprintf(stderr, "Error: unterminated string literal\n");
    exit(1);
}
```

Nested Comments: If a block comment is not properly terminated, a similar rule can be applied to ensure that the lexer does not enter an infinite loop:

```
<COMMENT><<EOF>> {
    fprintf(stderr, "Error: unterminated comment\n");
    exit(1);
}
```

By specifying error-handling behavior for particular contexts, you ensure that errors are caught as early as possible and reported in a meaningful way.

3.5.4 Logging and Debugging Errors

In addition to printing error messages, advanced error handling may involve logging errors to a file for later analysis. This is especially useful in production environments where debugging output must be preserved for diagnostic purposes:

```
{
    FILE *log = fopen("lexer_errors.log", "a");
    if (log) {
        fprintf(log, "Error: unexpected character '%s' at line %d\n", yytext, yylineno);
        fclose(log);
    }
    /* Continue processing or skip the character */
}
```

This approach ensures that error information is recorded persistently, aiding in long-term debugging and analysis.

3.5.5 Customizing Error Tokens

Some applications benefit from defining special error tokens that can be recognized by the parser. For instance, if the lexer encounters an error, it might return a token like LEX_ERROR to signal the parser that an error occurred:

```
{
    fprintf(stderr, "Lexical error: '%s'\n", yytext);
    return LEX_ERROR;
}
```

The parser can then include error productions to handle these tokens gracefully, perhaps by skipping to a synchronization point and attempting to resume parsing.

3.5.6 Testing Error Handling

Robust testing of error handling is essential:

- **Deliberate Malformed Input:** Create test cases that include common errors, such as missing quotes, unmatched delimiters, or invalid characters.
- **Edge Cases:** Test the boundaries, such as very long identifiers or numbers, to ensure that the lexer reports errors without crashing.
- **Stress Testing:** Run the lexer on large files with intentional errors to observe how it behaves under load and ensure that error messages remain clear and useful.

By rigorously testing error handling, you ensure that your lexer remains robust in the face of unexpected or malformed input.

3.6 Best Practices and Future Considerations

The advanced features of FLEX open up a world of possibilities for building sophisticated lexers. However, with great power comes great responsibility. Adopting best practices is essential for maintaining clarity, performance, and robustness.

3.6.1 Maintainability and Modularity

- **Modular Code Organization:** Organize your FLEX specifications into well-defined sections. Use macros to encapsulate recurring patterns and functions to handle complex actions. This modularity makes your code easier to read, test, and maintain.
- **Clear Documentation:** Comment your FLEX file thoroughly. Explain the purpose of start conditions, the reasoning behind complex regular expressions, and the expected behavior of error-handling routines.
- **Consistent Naming Conventions:** Use consistent and descriptive names for macros, functions, and tokens. This consistency helps prevent confusion and errors when the specification grows in size.

3.6.2 Performance and Optimization

- **Efficient Regular Expressions:** Optimize your regular expressions to minimize backtracking and reduce processing time. Test different patterns to see which performs best for your specific input.
- **Buffer Management:** Fine-tune the internal buffering settings if you process very large files. Adjusting buffer sizes can have a significant impact on performance.
- **Minimizing Dynamic Memory Allocation:** Reuse allocated memory where possible and be vigilant about freeing resources to avoid memory leaks.

3.6.3 Robust Error Recovery

- **Comprehensive Error Handling:** Ensure that every unexpected condition is handled gracefully. Do not allow a single error to cascade and cause the entire lexical analysis to fail.
- **User-Friendly Messages:** Provide error messages that are clear, specific, and actionable. Include context, such as line numbers and the problematic input, to help users quickly locate and fix issues.
- **Testing and Validation:** Regularly test your error-handling routines with a variety of malformed inputs to ensure they perform as expected.

3.6.4 Future Directions in Lexical Analysis

While FLEX remains a robust and widely used tool, the field of lexical analysis continues to evolve. Future trends may include:

- **Incremental Lexing:** For applications such as IDEs, incremental lexing—updating only the affected portions of the input—can improve responsiveness and performance.
- **Integration with Modern Languages:** While FLEX generates C code, new tools and libraries may offer better integration with high-level languages, enabling a smoother workflow in modern development environments.
- **Enhanced Error Correction:** Machine learning techniques might eventually be integrated into lexers to automatically suggest corrections or even auto-correct common errors.
- **Hybrid Approaches:** Combining traditional DFA-based lexing with probabilistic models could yield lexers that perform well even in the presence of noisy or ambiguous input.

By staying informed about these trends, you can ensure that your skills remain relevant and that your lexical analysis strategies continue to evolve.

3.7 Real-World Case Studies in Advanced FLEX Usage

To illustrate the advanced features of FLEX, consider the following real-world case studies that demonstrate how these techniques are applied in practice.

3.7.1 Case Study: A High-Performance Code Editor

A team developing a high-performance code editor used FLEX to build a lexer capable of handling complex source code with nested comments, string literals with escape sequences, and multiple contextual states. By employing start conditions for comments and strings, they were able to isolate processing for different parts of the source code, ensuring that errors in one section did not propagate to others. Advanced error handling routines provided detailed error messages, and performance optimizations—such as fine-tuning the input buffer size and optimizing regular expressions—resulted in a lexer that operated with minimal latency even on very large files.

3.7.2 Case Study: Processing Configuration Files in a Distributed System

In a distributed system requiring dynamic configuration, a robust lexer was built using FLEX to process configuration files. The lexer needed to handle various numeric formats, quoted strings with escaped characters, and inline comments. Using a combination of modular regular expressions and a comprehensive error-handling mechanism, the lexer ensured that malformed configurations were caught early, providing clear error messages that allowed administrators to correct issues swiftly. The integration with a symbol table further ensured that configuration parameters were tracked and validated against expected types.

3.7.3 Case Study: Building a Domain-Specific Language (DSL)

A software development team created a DSL for financial modeling, where the syntax allowed for complex expressions, special currency formats, and embedded comments. The FLEX specification was designed with extensive use of macros for digits, letters, and currency symbols. Start conditions were employed to handle multi-line comments and string literals with specific financial formatting rules. Additionally, the team integrated a custom error recovery strategy that logged errors to a central system for real-time monitoring. This robust lexer, built with FLEX, became the foundation for a complete DSL toolchain that enabled rapid prototyping and iteration.

Chapter 4: Understanding YACC – A Parser Generator

YACC, an acronym for "Yet Another Compiler Compiler," is one of the foundational tools in compiler design and language processing. Over the decades, it has evolved into a robust utility that translates a high-level description of a language grammar into a working parser. This chapter provides an in-depth exploration of YACC, from its historical background and theoretical underpinnings to the nuts and bolts of constructing a YACC program and integrating it into a build process. The following sections will guide you through every essential concept, making it possible for you to leverage YACC effectively in real-world projects.

4.1 Introduction to YACC

YACC emerged from the pioneering days of Unix development, where efficient tools for automating compiler construction were in high demand. Developed initially at Bell Labs, YACC was designed to simplify the process of developing a compiler by generating the parser automatically from a formal grammar. This innovation helped reduce the manual coding of complex parsing routines, thus streamlining the creation of language interpreters and compilers.

Historical Context and Purpose

The late 1970s and early 1980s witnessed a surge in the creation of programming languages and the need for efficient compiler construction methods. At this time, the manual implementation of parsers was both error-prone and time-consuming. YACC was conceived as a tool to automatically generate parsers from context-free grammars (CFGs), offering a systematic and repeatable approach to handle the syntax of programming languages.

YACC's design was influenced by the work of Noam Chomsky on formal grammars, and its implementation leveraged well-established parsing techniques such as LALR (Look-Ahead LR) parsing. Its ability to handle ambiguous grammars, assign precedence, and manage errors efficiently made it a popular choice among developers and academic institutions alike. By abstracting away many of the tedious aspects of parser construction, YACC allowed developers to focus on higher-level aspects of language design and semantic analysis.

The Role of YACC in Compiler Construction

At its core, YACC takes a grammar specification as input and produces source code for a parser, typically written in the C programming language. The parser generated by YACC reads the tokens produced by a lexical analyzer (often generated by a tool like FLEX) and determines whether the input conforms to the defined grammar. This separation of concerns—where lexical analysis and syntactic parsing are handled by separate tools—has become a standard approach in compiler design.

In many modern compiler projects, YACC plays a critical role by serving as the bridge between the lexical analysis phase and semantic interpretation. It enables developers to define grammatical rules in a readable, maintainable format while automatically generating the corresponding parsing code. As a result, YACC remains a powerful educational and practical tool, used extensively to introduce students and professionals to compiler theory and practice.

Benefits and Limitations

One of the primary benefits of YACC is its ability to handle complex grammars with minimal manual intervention. By leveraging LALR parsing techniques, YACC can resolve many ambiguities that arise in language definitions. Furthermore, its integration with C allows for seamless embedding of semantic actions—code snippets that execute when a rule is matched—making it possible to construct abstract syntax trees (ASTs), perform semantic checks, or even generate intermediate code.

However, YACC also has its limitations. Its error messages, while functional, can sometimes be cryptic, making debugging a challenge, especially for beginners. Additionally, the rigid structure of YACC programs may require developers to invest time in understanding its nuances, particularly regarding how precedence and associativity are declared and managed. Despite these challenges, the benefits of automation and structured grammar specification often outweigh the difficulties, especially in large-scale projects where consistency and maintainability are paramount.

Practical Applications

Beyond academic exercises, YACC has been employed in numerous real-world projects. From constructing simple interpreters for domain-specific languages to serving as the backbone of full-scale compilers for general-purpose programming languages, YACC's influence is widespread. Its design principles have also inspired many modern parser generators, making it a cornerstone in the evolution of compiler technology.

In summary, this introductory section has set the stage for a deeper exploration of YACC. With its historical roots, practical advantages, and inherent limitations laid out, we now transition into the theoretical framework that underpins YACC's operation: context-free grammars and parsing.

4.2 Context-Free Grammars and Parsing

A comprehensive understanding of YACC cannot be achieved without a solid grounding in the theory of context-free grammars (CFGs) and the parsing techniques that operate on them. This section explores the formal definitions, practical examples, and the parsing strategies that YACC employs, offering a detailed look at the theoretical concepts that guide its design.

Fundamentals of Context-Free Grammars

A context-free grammar is a formal system used to describe the syntax of programming languages and other formal languages. In a CFG, the language is defined by a set of production rules that describe how symbols can be combined to form valid strings. A CFG consists of:

- **Terminals:** The basic symbols from which strings are formed. In programming languages, these could be keywords, operators, or identifiers.
- **Non-Terminals:** Symbols that represent abstract syntactic categories, such as expressions or statements.
- **Production Rules:** The rules that describe how non-terminals can be replaced by combinations of terminals and other non-terminals.
- **Start Symbol:** A special non-terminal from which parsing begins.

For example, consider a simple grammar for arithmetic expressions:

```
Expr   → Expr '+' Term | Term
Term   → Term '*' Factor | Factor
Factor → '(' Expr ')' | number
```

In this grammar, **Expr**, **Term**, and **Factor** are non-terminals, while '+', '*', '(', ')', and **number** are terminals. This CFG defines the structure of arithmetic expressions, specifying how operators and operands can be combined.

Parsing Techniques and Their Importance

Parsing is the process of analyzing a sequence of tokens to determine its grammatical structure according to a given CFG. In essence, the parser constructs a parse tree (or derivation tree) that represents the syntactic structure of the input. There are several parsing techniques, but YACC is particularly known for using LALR (Look-Ahead LR) parsing.

LR Parsing

LR parsers, including their LALR variants, are bottom-up parsers. They work by reading the input from left to right and constructing the parse tree in a bottom-up manner. The "L" stands for left-to-right scanning of the input, "R" for constructing a rightmost derivation in reverse, and "LA" for the use of look-ahead tokens to resolve ambiguities.

The strength of LR parsing lies in its ability to handle a large class of grammars, including those that are ambiguous or have left-recursive productions. YACC takes advantage of these strengths to generate parsers that can efficiently process complex language constructs.

Ambiguity and Grammar Conflicts

A significant challenge in parsing is dealing with ambiguity—situations where a single string can be derived in multiple ways from the grammar. Ambiguity often leads to conflicts during the parsing process, such as shift/reduce or reduce/reduce conflicts. YACC provides mechanisms to resolve these conflicts through the declaration of precedence and associativity rules. By assigning a hierarchy to operators and specifying whether they are left- or right-associative, YACC can systematically resolve ambiguities that arise during parsing.

For instance, in arithmetic expressions, the ambiguity between multiplication and addition is resolved by declaring that multiplication has higher precedence than addition. Similarly, the associativity of the subtraction operator (usually left-associative) is specified to ensure that expressions are grouped correctly.

Constructing the Parse Tree

The parse tree is a hierarchical representation of the input string according to the grammar rules. Each node in the tree corresponds to a grammar symbol, and the structure of the tree reflects the nested relationships defined by the production rules. In practice, the parse tree serves as an intermediate representation that can be used for further semantic analysis or code generation.

YACC leverages the parse tree construction process to allow developers to embed semantic actions within the grammar rules. These actions are snippets of code (typically in C) that execute when a particular rule is applied. They can be used to build an abstract syntax tree (AST), perform type checking, or even generate intermediate code for later stages of the compiler.

Error Detection and Recovery

Another critical aspect of parsing is error detection and recovery. A robust parser must not only recognize valid input but also handle syntax errors gracefully. YACC offers facilities to manage errors through specialized error productions and recovery routines. When the parser encounters an error, it can invoke user-defined error-handling code to report the problem, attempt to resynchronize with the input, or even recover by skipping erroneous tokens.

The design of error-handling routines in YACC requires careful consideration. The goal is to provide meaningful error messages that can guide developers in correcting their code, while also ensuring that the parser can continue processing subsequent input. In many cases, the error-handling code may involve logging the error, providing hints for correction, or even attempting to parse a default construct in place of the erroneous one.

Theoretical Foundations in Practice

The theoretical underpinnings of context-free grammars and parsing are not merely academic—they have practical implications in the design of YACC. The tool's ability to generate efficient, reliable parsers is a direct consequence of its grounding in formal language theory. By understanding the principles of CFGs and the mechanics of LR parsing, developers can craft grammars that are both expressive and unambiguous, thereby reducing the likelihood of conflicts during parser generation.

Moreover, the interplay between theory and practice in YACC provides valuable insights into language design. For example, the need to resolve ambiguities often leads to better-designed languages with clear operator hierarchies and well-defined syntactic constructs. In this way, YACC not only aids in parser construction but also contributes to the evolution of programming language design as a whole.

In conclusion, this section has laid the groundwork for understanding how YACC leverages context-free grammars and advanced parsing techniques to generate powerful parsers. With these concepts firmly in place, we now turn our attention to the structure of a YACC program itself.

4.3 Structure of a YACC Program

A YACC program is structured in a way that clearly separates the grammar definitions, parsing rules, and supporting code. This organization facilitates the creation of maintainable and modular parser code. In this section, we explore the typical layout of a YACC file, explaining the purpose of each section and how they work together to form a cohesive parser.

Overall Layout and Delimiters

A YACC source file is typically divided into three main sections, each separated by the delimiter %%. These sections are:

1. **The Definitions Section:** This area is used to declare tokens, define macros, and include any necessary header files or declarations.
2. **The Rules Section:** This is the core of the YACC program, where the grammar rules and corresponding actions are defined.
3. **The User Code Section:** Placed after the second delimiter, this section contains auxiliary C code, including function definitions and helper routines that support the parser's operation.

Each section plays a distinct role in the overall operation of the parser. The clear separation of these components allows developers to focus on one aspect of the parser at a time, improving both clarity and maintainability.

The Definitions Section

In the definitions section, you begin by including necessary header files and defining tokens. Tokens represent the basic elements of your language—such as keywords, identifiers, and operators—that will be produced by the lexical analyzer. For example:

```
%{
#include <stdio.h>
#include "y.tab.h"
%}


%token NUMBER IDENTIFIER
%token PLUS MINUS MULTIPLY DIVIDE
%left '+' '-'
%left '*' '/'
```

Here, the %{ %} block encloses C code that is copied directly into the generated parser source file. It typically includes header files and any declarations needed by the semantic actions. The %token declarations define the tokens that the parser will recognize. Additionally, the %left directives set the associativity for operators, ensuring that expressions are parsed correctly.

This section may also contain macro definitions, global variables, and declarations that will be used throughout the YACC program. It is important to keep this section clean and well-organized, as it lays the groundwork for the rules that follow.

The Rules Section

The rules section is where the grammar of your language is defined. It consists of a series of production rules that describe how the non-terminal symbols of your grammar can be expanded into sequences of terminal and non-terminal symbols. Each production rule can be associated with an action—written in C—that executes when the rule is applied.

A simple example of a rule in this section might look like:

```
expr: expr '+' term { $$ = $1 + $3; }
   | term { $$ = $1; }
   ;
```

In this example, the non-terminal expr is defined by two production rules. The first rule indicates that an expr can be formed by an expr followed by a '+' and a term, with the corresponding action performing an addition. The second rule defines an `expr` simply as a `term`. The semantic value of a rule is represented by the special symbol $$, while the values of individual symbols on the right-hand side of the rule are accessed by $1, $2, and so on.

The rules section is the heart of a YACC program, translating the abstract definitions of a language into concrete instructions for constructing the parse tree. It is here that the interplay between syntax and semantics is most evident. Developers can insert custom C code to perform semantic actions such as constructing AST nodes, checking types, or even initiating code generation for later compiler stages.

The User Code Section

The final section of a YACC file contains user-defined C code that is appended to the end of the generated parser file. This section is ideal for placing auxiliary functions, error-handling routines, and any other support code that the parser might require.

For example, you might define an error reporting function:

```
void yyerror(const char *s) {
    fprintf(stderr, "Syntax error: %s\n", s);
}
```

This function is invoked by the parser whenever it encounters an error. Placing such code in the user code section ensures that it is available to the parser without cluttering the main grammar definitions. It also allows for more modular development, where the parsing logic remains separate from the error handling and utility functions.

Integration with the Lexical Analyzer

One of the critical aspects of a YACC program is its interaction with a lexical analyzer. Although the lexical analyzer is usually generated by a tool such as FLEX, the YACC file must provide a clear interface for receiving tokens. Typically, the lexical analyzer function `yylex()` is declared in the definitions section or is included through a header file. When the parser calls `yylex()`, it expects to receive the next token from the input stream along with its semantic value.

This integration ensures that the responsibilities of lexical analysis and parsing remain distinct, yet they work in concert to process the input. The tokens produced by the lexical analyzer are then matched against the grammar rules defined in the rules section. This separation of concerns not only improves code clarity but also allows each component to be developed and tested independently.

Example of a Complete YACC Program Structure

To illustrate the structure, consider the following simplified YACC program for a basic arithmetic parser:

```
%{
#include <stdio.h>
#include <stdlib.h>
void yyerror(const char *);
int yylex(void);
%}


%token NUMBER
%left '+' '-'
%left '*' '/'


%%
expr: expr '+' expr { $$ = $1 + $3; }
   | expr '-' expr { $$ = $1 - $3; }
   | expr '*' expr { $$ = $1 * $3; }
   | expr '/' expr { $$ = $1 / $3; }
   | '(' expr ')'  { $$ = $2; }
   | NUMBER        { $$ = $1; }
   ;
%%


void yyerror(const char *s) {
    fprintf(stderr, "Error: %s\n", s);
}


int main(void) {
    printf("Enter an expression: ");
    yyparse();
    return 0;
}
```

This example demonstrates the clear segmentation of a YACC program. The definitions section includes necessary headers and token declarations, the rules section contains the grammar and associated actions, and the user code section provides the error-handling function and the `main` function. Notice how each section plays a vital role in creating a cohesive parser.

Best Practices for Organizing YACC Files

To maximize maintainability and readability, consider the following best practices when structuring a YACC program:

- **Keep the Definitions Section Concise:** Limit the inclusion of external dependencies and declarations to what is strictly necessary for the parser.

- **Modularize Semantic Actions:** Where possible, delegate complex semantic actions to helper functions rather than embedding lengthy code within the rules section.
- **Document Production Rules:** Include comments that explain the intent behind each production rule, especially for grammars that are non-trivial or contain workarounds for ambiguity.
- **Isolate Error Handling:** Develop comprehensive error-handling routines and keep them separate from the main parsing logic to facilitate easier debugging and maintenance.
- **Maintain Consistency:** Use a consistent naming convention for tokens, non-terminals, and semantic variables to reduce confusion and potential errors during development.

With a solid grasp of the structure of a YACC program, we can now proceed to examine the finer details of how tokens, grammar rules, and semantic actions are defined and utilized.

4.4 Defining Tokens, Rules, and Actions

The core of any YACC program lies in the precise definition of tokens, grammar rules, and the semantic actions that drive the parsing process. This section provides a detailed exploration of each of these components, explaining how they interact to form a powerful parser generator.

Tokens: The Building Blocks of Grammar

Tokens are the smallest units of meaning in the language you are trying to parse. They are usually produced by a lexical analyzer and represent keywords, identifiers, literals, operators, and other syntactic elements. In YACC, tokens are declared in the definitions section using the %token directive. For example:

```
%token NUMBER IDENTIFIER IF ELSE WHILE RETURN
```

Each token declaration assigns a unique numerical code to the token, which the parser uses to identify it during parsing. It is crucial to ensure that the token definitions in your YACC file are consistent with those generated by your lexical analyzer. Mismatches in token definitions can lead to runtime errors or misinterpretation of the input.

Establishing Operator Precedence and Associativity

In languages that include arithmetic or logical operators, defining operator precedence and associativity is essential for resolving ambiguities in expressions. YACC allows you to declare these attributes using directives such as %left, %right, and %nonassoc. For example:

```
%left '+' '-'
%left '*' '/'
```

These declarations instruct YACC on how to handle expressions with multiple operators. The precedence rules ensure that multiplication and division are evaluated before addition and subtraction, while the associativity rules dictate the order of evaluation for operators with the same precedence level. This is particularly important in expressions where the order of operations is not explicitly indicated by parentheses.

Defining Grammar Rules

Grammar rules in YACC specify how tokens and non-terminals combine to form higher-level language constructs. Each rule is composed of a left-hand side (a non-terminal symbol) and a right-hand side (a sequence of tokens and/or non-terminals) separated by a colon. For example:

```
statement: IF '(' expression ')' statement
    | IF '(' expression ')' statement ELSE statement
    | expression ';'
    ;
```

In this example, the non-terminal statement is defined by three production rules. The first two rules handle conditional statements, with and without an else clause, while the third rule defines a statement as a simple expression terminated by a semicolon. The careful design of these rules is critical to accurately representing the language's syntax and ensuring that the parser can recognize all valid constructs.

Embedding Semantic Actions

Semantic actions are C code snippets that are executed when a particular production rule is matched. They are enclosed in curly braces immediately following the rule. These actions typically perform tasks such as constructing parts of the abstract syntax tree (AST), performing type checking, or initiating code generation. Consider the following rule for a simple arithmetic expression:

```
expr: expr '+' term { $$ = $1 + $3; }
    | term { $$ = $1; }
    ;
```

In this rule, the action { $$ = $1 + $3; } specifies that when the parser matches the pattern expr '+' term, it should compute the sum of the semantic values of the left-hand side expression ($1) and the term ($3), and store the result in the semantic value of the current rule ($$). The semantic values, represented by these special symbols, provide a mechanism to pass information between rules. They are essential for constructing complex data structures like ASTs that represent the parsed input.

Semantic Value Types and YYSTYPE

YACC uses the symbol YYSTYPE to define the type of semantic values associated with tokens and non-terminals. By default, YYSTYPE is typically defined as an integer, but it can be redefined to a union or structure to support more complex data. For example, in a language that requires both integer values and pointers to tree nodes, you might define YYSTYPE as follows:

```
typedef union {
    int intval;
    struct ast_node *node;
} YYSTYPE;
```

After redefining YYSTYPE, you need to inform YACC about the new definition. This allows semantic actions to access and manipulate the data in a type-safe manner. Properly defining YYSTYPE is crucial for ensuring that the semantic actions can perform the required computations and data manipulations without type errors.

Advanced Techniques in Semantic Actions

Semantic actions can be used to implement a wide range of functionalities beyond simple arithmetic computations. For instance, they can be employed to build and traverse ASTs, perform symbol table lookups, and enforce semantic rules of the language. One advanced technique is to use semantic actions to implement type checking. Consider a rule for an assignment statement:

```
assignment: IDENTIFIER '=' expression {
    if (!check_type($1, $3)) {
        yyerror("Type mismatch in assignment");
    }
    $$ = create_assignment_node($1, $3);
}
;
```

In this example, the semantic action calls a hypothetical check_type() function to ensure that the types on both sides of the assignment are compatible. If a type mismatch is detected, an error is reported using yyerror(). Otherwise, an assignment node is created in the AST. This approach illustrates how semantic actions bridge the gap between syntactic structure and the semantic meaning of the language.

Modularizing and Organizing Semantic Code

Given that semantic actions can become quite complex, it is often beneficial to modularize the code they invoke. Instead of embedding extensive C code directly within the grammar rules, you can call external functions that are defined in the user code section or in separate source files. This not only improves readability but also makes the code more maintainable. For example:

```
expr: expr '+' term { $$ = add_expressions($1, $3); }
   | term { $$ = $1; }
   ;
```

Here, the semantic action delegates the addition operation to a helper function add_expressions(). This modular approach allows you to isolate complex logic and test it independently of the parser, which is especially useful in larger projects.

Handling Ambiguities with Semantic Actions

Ambiguities in grammar rules can sometimes lead to conflicts during parser generation. YACC provides mechanisms to resolve these ambiguities by allowing semantic actions to specify which alternative to choose in case of a conflict. For instance, when dealing with expressions that can be parsed in multiple ways, you may design your semantic actions to incorporate additional context or precedence rules to ensure that the correct interpretation is chosen.

In more advanced scenarios, you might use semantic actions to implement error recovery strategies. This involves designing the actions to detect when a particular sequence of tokens does not match any valid production and then attempting to recover gracefully. Such techniques can significantly improve the robustness of your parser in the face of unexpected or malformed input.

4.5 Running YACC: Compilation and Execution

Having developed a complete YACC program with well-defined tokens, grammar rules, and semantic actions, the next logical step is to understand how to compile and execute the parser. This section covers everything from the initial invocation of YACC to the final execution of the generated parser, including tips for debugging and performance optimization.

The YACC Invocation Process

The first step in running a YACC program is to invoke the YACC tool itself. This is typically done via the command line. When you run YACC on your source file, it reads the grammar specifications and produces a C source file (commonly named y.tab.c) that contains the parser code. A typical command might look like:

```
yacc -d myparser.y
```

The -d flag instructs YACC to generate a header file (usually y.tab.h) that contains token definitions. This header file is essential when integrating the parser with a lexical analyzer, ensuring that both components share the same token definitions.

Compiling the Generated Parser

Once YACC has generated the parser source file, the next step is to compile it using a C compiler such as GCC. The compilation step usually involves linking the generated parser with the object files or libraries corresponding to the lexical analyzer. For example:

```
gcc -o myparser y.tab.c lex.yy.c -ll
```

In this command, lex.yy.c is the source file generated by a lexical analyzer tool (such as FLEX), and -ll links the lex library. It is important to ensure that all dependencies are correctly linked to avoid runtime errors.

Integrating with the Build Process

In larger projects, integrating YACC into an automated build process is crucial. Tools like Make can be used to automate the generation and compilation of YACC files. A simple Makefile might include rules such as:

```
parser: y.tab.c lex.yy.c
        gcc -o parser y.tab.c lex.yy.c -ll


y.tab.c y.tab.h: myparser.y
        yacc -d myparser.y


lex.yy.c: mylexer.l y.tab.h
        flex mylexer.l
```

This Makefile ensures that changes to the YACC or FLEX files automatically trigger the regeneration of the necessary source files, streamlining the development process.

Debugging the Parser

Even with a well-defined grammar and carefully written semantic actions, errors may still occur. YACC provides several debugging options that can be enabled during parser generation or at runtime. For example, you can compile the generated parser with debugging symbols:

```
gcc -g -o myparser y.tab.c lex.yy.c -ll
```

During execution, you can use the yydebug variable to print detailed trace information. Setting yydebug to a non-zero value will cause the parser to output debugging information, such as the state transitions and token consumption:

```
int main(void) {
    yydebug = 1;
    yyparse();
    return 0;
}
```

This detailed output can be invaluable in diagnosing parsing conflicts, understanding the decision-making process of the parser, and ultimately refining the grammar.

Performance Optimization

While YACC-generated parsers are generally efficient, there are scenarios where performance optimization is necessary, particularly in systems that process large volumes of input. Some strategies for performance improvement include:

- **Optimizing Grammar Rules:** Simplifying rules to reduce ambiguity and eliminate unnecessary recursion can lead to more efficient parsing.
- **Minimizing Semantic Action Overhead:** Where possible, streamline semantic actions to reduce the amount of computation performed during parsing.
- **Memory Management:** Ensure that memory allocation and deallocation in semantic actions are efficient and avoid memory leaks. Using pooling or other memory management strategies can improve overall performance.
- **Profiling the Parser:** Tools such as gprof can be used to profile the parser, identifying bottlenecks in both the parsing and semantic action code.

By carefully analyzing the performance characteristics of your YACC-generated parser, you can identify opportunities for optimization that lead to faster, more responsive applications.

Handling Runtime Errors

Error handling is a critical component of any robust parser. YACC provides mechanisms to detect syntax errors and recover from them gracefully. When the parser encounters an unexpected token, it calls the yyerror () function, which should be implemented by the developer. A robust yyerror () function not only reports the error but can also provide context, such as the line number and a snippet of the problematic input.

```
void yyerror(const char *s) {
    fprintf(stderr, "Error at line %d: %s\n", yylineno, s);
}
```

In addition to error reporting, some advanced YACC programs implement error recovery strategies. This might involve inserting a default token, skipping tokens until a known state is reached, or even resynchronizing based on a specific delimiter. These strategies help the parser continue processing the remainder of the input, which is particularly useful in interactive systems or compilers that must report multiple errors in a single run.

Testing and Validation

A well-constructed parser should be accompanied by a comprehensive suite of tests. Testing a YACC-generated parser involves feeding it a variety of input strings—both valid and invalid—to ensure that it correctly recognizes the grammar and handles errors gracefully. Unit tests can be written to validate the semantic actions and the construction of the abstract syntax tree, while integration tests ensure that the entire pipeline, from lexical analysis to semantic processing, functions as intended.

Automated testing frameworks can be integrated into your build process, ensuring that any changes to the grammar or semantic actions do not inadvertently break existing functionality. Regression tests are particularly valuable when the language evolves or when new features are added.

Case Studies and Practical Examples

To illustrate the full process of running YACC—from source file creation to parser execution—consider the following case study. Suppose you are developing a parser for a simple scripting language. The language includes arithmetic expressions, variable assignments, and conditional statements. Your YACC file, `script_parser.y`, is designed to capture these constructs using the techniques described earlier.

After writing the grammar rules and embedding the necessary semantic actions, you invoke YACC to generate `y.tab.c` and `y.tab.h`. Next, you compile these files along with the output from your lexical analyzer (`lex.yy.c`) using GCC. During testing, you encounter a few syntax errors in the input script. By enabling debugging (`yydebug = 1`) and carefully examining the trace output, you pinpoint the problematic rules. With the errors fixed, you recompile and run the parser, which now successfully constructs an AST representing the script. This end-to-end process not only demonstrates the practical application of YACC but also highlights the iterative nature of developing reliable language processing tools.

Advanced Configuration Options

YACC offers several command-line options and configuration settings that allow developers to fine-tune the behavior of the generated parser. Some options include:

- **-v Option:** Generates an output file (`y.output`) that contains detailed information about the parser's state machine. This file is invaluable for diagnosing conflicts and understanding the internal workings of the parser.
- **Custom Stack Sizes:** In scenarios where the parser must handle very deep recursion (such as in languages with deeply nested structures), it may be necessary to adjust the size of the parsing stack. Custom stack sizes can be set at compile time or via runtime parameters.
- **Integration with Other Tools:** YACC can be integrated with other language processing tools, such as debuggers or profilers. For instance, when combined with a tool like GDB, you can step through the parser's execution to gain a deeper understanding of how it processes input.

By leveraging these advanced options, developers can optimize the parser for specific use cases, ensuring both efficiency and robustness.

Chapter 5: Syntax-Directed Translation in YACC

Syntax-directed translation is an essential paradigm in compiler design where the syntax (grammar) of a language is augmented with semantic actions. These actions, embedded within the grammar rules, perform computations, build abstract representations, and even generate target code as the parser recognizes valid constructs in the source language. YACC, being a parser generator with embedded C code support, is an excellent tool for implementing syntax-directed translation. This chapter explains how to leverage YACC for translating syntactic structures into semantic outcomes, enabling the creation of efficient compilers, interpreters, and language processors.

5.1 Associativity and Operator Precedence

Introduction to Operator Handling

One of the core challenges in language parsing is dealing with operators—symbols that perform operations such as addition, subtraction, multiplication, and division. In many programming languages, these operators must be evaluated in a specific order, defined by their precedence (the order in which operations are performed) and associativity (the order in which operators of the same precedence are processed). In YACC, handling these nuances is achieved by explicitly declaring associativity and precedence within the grammar file.

The Rationale Behind Precedence and Associativity

When parsing expressions, a naive approach might attempt to derive every possible interpretation, but this quickly becomes unmanageable with even modest complexity. For example, consider the expression:

```
a - b - c
```

Without any guidelines, it is ambiguous whether the intended evaluation is (a−b)−c(a - b) - c or a−(b−c)a - (b - c). By defining subtraction as left-associative, YACC can unambiguously determine that the expression should be parsed as (a−b)−c(a - b) - c. Operator precedence further ensures that in expressions like:

```
a + b * c
```

the multiplication is performed before the addition, leading to the correct evaluation as a+(b*c)a + (b * c).

Specifying Associativity in YACC

In YACC, associativity is specified using directives such as %left, %right, and %nonassoc at the beginning of the file. These directives assign associativity properties to the operators, making the grammar easier to read and less prone to conflicts. For example:

```
%left '+' '-'
%left '*' '/'
```

This snippet tells YACC that the plus and minus operators are left-associative and have lower precedence than multiplication and division, which are also left-associative by default. In the context of syntax-directed translation, these declarations help the semantic actions by ensuring that the parsed tree reflects the intended order of evaluation. By reducing ambiguity at the grammar level, the semantic actions can focus solely on building the correct computational structures without additional disambiguation logic.

Precedence Rules and Conflict Resolution

Despite the careful design of grammar rules, ambiguity is an ever-present challenge. YACC resolves conflicts by referring to the precedence and associativity rules provided in the definitions section. When the parser encounters a shift/reduce conflict—where it is unclear whether to shift the next token or reduce a production rule—the defined precedence and associativity values guide the decision-making process.

Consider a grammar fragment handling binary arithmetic expressions:

```
expr: expr '+' expr { $$ = $1 + $3; }
    | expr '*' expr { $$ = $1 * $3; }
    | NUMBER        { $$ = $1; }
    ;
```

Without precedence rules, the parser might be unable to determine the correct order in an expression like $3 + 4 * 5$. By adding precedence declarations:

```
%left '+'
%left '*'
```

YACC is informed that multiplication should bind more tightly than addition if specified in the correct order. This means that even if both productions could potentially apply, the parser will choose the rule that reflects the intended arithmetic order.

Impact on Semantic Translation

The careful assignment of precedence and associativity is not only a syntactic concern—it directly impacts how semantic actions are applied. When building abstract syntax trees or performing intermediate code generation, the parse tree must correctly represent the intended evaluation order. For instance, in constructing an AST for the expression $a + b * c$, a correct parse tree would show $*$ as a deeper node compared to $+$, reflecting that multiplication is evaluated before addition.

Thus, in YACC, the explicit declaration of operator precedence and associativity simplifies the semantic actions. It allows the developer to assume that when an arithmetic expression is reduced, it has already been disambiguated to reflect the true operator order. This foundational step ensures that subsequent translation steps, such as type checking and code generation, work on a sound semantic basis.

Advanced Operator Handling

In more complex languages, operators can sometimes be overloaded or have context-sensitive behaviors. YACC supports these advanced requirements by allowing more intricate declarations. For instance, you may have different operators with the same symbol but used in different contexts (e.g., the binary minus versus the unary negation operator). In such cases, you can use distinct tokens for each operator variant and specify unique precedence rules to differentiate their behavior. Semantic actions then use these tokens to decide on the appropriate translation strategy.

Furthermore, some languages support ternary operators or other multi-operand operators. YACC's mechanism for associativity and precedence can be extended to accommodate these constructs, albeit with additional semantic checks. The key idea remains: resolve ambiguity at the grammar level so that the semantic translation process is straightforward and consistent.

Practical Examples

Let's examine a practical example. Suppose you are implementing a simple calculator. You want to ensure that the expression $2 + 3 * 4 - 5$ is interpreted correctly. You could write your YACC declarations as follows:

```
%left '+' '-'
%left '*' '/'
%token NUMBER
```

```
%%
expr: expr '+' expr { $$ = $1 + $3; }
    | expr '-' expr { $$ = $1 - $3; }
    | expr '*' expr { $$ = $1 * $3; }
    | expr '/' expr {
        if($3 == 0) {
            yyerror("Division by zero");
            $$ = 0;
        } else {
            $$ = $1 / $3;
        }
    }
    | '(' expr ')'  { $$ = $2; }
    | NUMBER        { $$ = $1; }
    ;
%%
```

In this example, associativity and precedence are defined such that multiplication and division take precedence over addition and subtraction. The semantic actions directly perform the arithmetic, confident that the order of operations has already been correctly enforced by the parser.

5.2 Abstract Syntax Trees (ASTs)

Introduction to ASTs

An Abstract Syntax Tree (AST) is a fundamental data structure in compiler design that represents the hierarchical syntactic structure of the source code. Unlike concrete syntax trees, which capture every detail of the input, ASTs abstract away unnecessary syntactic elements to focus on the core semantic relationships. In the context of syntax-directed translation, ASTs serve as the backbone for further processing such as semantic analysis, optimization, and code generation.

Building ASTs in YACC

YACC enables the construction of ASTs by allowing you to embed semantic actions directly within grammar rules. These actions typically involve creating nodes for the AST and linking them together according to the structure of the input. Each node in the AST might represent constructs such as operators, literals, identifiers, or even entire statements.

Consider the following simplified grammar rule for an arithmetic expression:

```
expr: expr '+' expr { $$ = create_node("+", $1, $3); }
    | expr '*' expr { $$ = create_node("*", $1, $3); }
    | NUMBER        { $$ = create_leaf($1); }
    ;
```

In this example, the semantic actions call helper functions such as create_node and create_leaf to build the AST. The function create_node takes an operator and two subtrees, combining them into a new AST node that represents an operation. The create_leaf function handles terminal nodes, typically numeric values or identifiers.

Defining AST Node Structures

Before you can build an AST, you need to define the data structure for an AST node. This is typically done in a header file or within the user code section of your YACC file. A common approach is to define a structure that contains the type of node, pointers to child nodes, and possibly additional information like token values or line numbers. For example:

```
typedef enum { NODE_OPERATOR, NODE_NUMBER, NODE_IDENTIFIER } NodeType;


typedef struct ast_node {
    NodeType type;
    char *value;            // For operator symbols or identifiers
    int number;             // For numeric literals
    struct ast_node *left;   // Left child for binary operations
    struct ast_node *right;   // Right child for binary operations
} ASTNode;
```

With such a definition, the helper functions used in the semantic actions can allocate and initialize nodes appropriately. For instance, create_node might allocate a new ASTNode, assign the operator symbol to the node's value, and link the left and right subtrees.

Semantic Actions for AST Construction

The real power of syntax-directed translation comes into play when semantic actions build the AST dynamically as the parser recognizes the input. Consider a more complex example where you have to handle nested expressions and operator hierarchies. The semantic actions might look like this:

```
expr: expr '+' term {
        ASTNode *node = create_node("+", $1, $3);
        $$ = node;
    }
    | term { $$ = $1; }
    ;


term: term '*' factor {
        ASTNode *node = create_node("*", $1, $3);
```

```
    $$ = node;
  }
  | factor { $$ = $1; }
  ;


factor: '(' expr ')' { $$ = $2; }
   | NUMBER { $$ = create_leaf($1); }
   ;
```

In this grammar, each time an arithmetic operation is recognized, an AST node is created to represent that operation. The AST structure naturally reflects the precedence and associativity defined earlier, ensuring that the tree mirrors the intended evaluation order.

Benefits of Using ASTs

ASTs offer several advantages in the syntax-directed translation process:

- **Abstraction:** They abstract away syntactic details that are not relevant for further semantic analysis. For instance, parentheses used solely for grouping in the source code are not represented in the AST, as their effect is already captured by the tree structure.
- **Modularity:** ASTs provide a modular representation of the program, making it easier to apply transformations, optimizations, or analyses on specific parts of the code.
- **Interoperability:** Many compiler phases, including semantic analysis, optimization, and code generation, operate on ASTs. By constructing a well-formed AST, you facilitate these subsequent stages.
- **Error Reporting:** AST nodes can carry metadata such as line numbers or source code fragments. This information is invaluable when reporting semantic errors or warnings during later phases of compilation.

Traversal and Manipulation of ASTs

Once constructed, ASTs are typically traversed using tree traversal algorithms such as pre-order, in-order, or post-order traversal. Each traversal order can be useful for different purposes. For example, a post-order traversal is often used in code generation because it ensures that child expressions are processed before their parent operator, which is crucial for generating correct evaluation order in target code.

In YACC-based projects, you might integrate the AST traversal directly into the semantic actions or, more commonly, delegate the traversal to separate functions defined in the user code section. These functions can walk the AST to perform type checking, optimization, or generate intermediate code.

Advanced AST Construction Techniques

For languages with more complex syntax, the AST construction process may involve handling multiple types of nodes and even supporting polymorphic behavior. Techniques such as node decoration (attaching additional attributes to AST nodes) and the use of unions or variant types for semantic values become important. These techniques allow the AST to represent a wide range of language constructs while still being amenable to systematic traversal and transformation.

For example, in a language that supports function declarations, control structures, and expressions, the AST node structure might be extended as follows:

```c
typedef enum {
    NODE_OPERATOR,
    NODE_NUMBER,
    NODE_IDENTIFIER,
    NODE_FUNCTION_DECL,
    NODE_STATEMENT
} NodeType;


typedef struct ast_node {
    NodeType type;
    char *value;
    int number;
    struct ast_node *left;
    struct ast_node *right;
    // Additional fields for function declarations or statements
    struct ast_node *arguments;
    struct ast_node *body;
} ASTNode;
```

By carefully designing your AST node structures, you can ensure that every syntactic construct in your language is represented in a way that facilitates further semantic translation.

Case Study: Building an AST for a Mini Language

To illustrate the power of AST construction through syntax-directed translation, let's consider a case study. Imagine you are designing a mini programming language that supports variable assignments, arithmetic expressions, and conditional statements. The goal is to build an AST that can later be used for both semantic analysis and code generation.

A fragment of the YACC grammar for this mini language might look like:

```
program: statement_list { $$ = create_program_node($1); }
    ;
```

```
statement_list: statement_list statement { $$ = append_statement($1, $2); }
        | statement { $$ = create_statement_list($1); }
        ;


statement: IDENTIFIER '=' expr ';' {
        $$ = create_assignment_node($1, $3);
    }
    | IF '(' expr ')' statement {
        $$ = create_if_node($3, $5, NULL);
    }
    | IF '(' expr ')' statement ELSE statement {
        $$ = create_if_node($3, $5, $7);
    }
    ;
```

In this example, semantic actions call functions like `create_program_node`, `append_statement`, and `create_assignment_node` to build the AST. Notice how each non-terminal is associated with a semantic action that builds a subtree, eventually composing the entire program structure. This modular approach not only makes the grammar more readable but also simplifies subsequent phases such as code generation.

5.3 Parsing Arithmetic Expressions

The Importance of Arithmetic Expression Parsing

Arithmetic expressions are ubiquitous in programming languages, and parsing them correctly is critical for both correctness and efficiency. Syntax-directed translation in YACC shines in this domain by allowing you to not only validate arithmetic expressions but also to translate them into intermediate representations or direct computations.

Grammar Design for Arithmetic Expressions

The design of the grammar for arithmetic expressions is a delicate balance between clarity and correctness. A typical arithmetic expression grammar must account for the natural hierarchy of operations, handle parentheses correctly, and resolve potential ambiguities. Consider the following production rules:

```
expr: expr '+' term { $$ = create_node("+", $1, $3); }
    | expr '-' term { $$ = create_node("-", $1, $3); }
    | term       { $$ = $1; }
    ;
```

```
term: term '*' factor { $$ = create_node("*", $1, $3); }
    | term '/' factor { $$ = create_node("/", $1, $3); }
    | factor          { $$ = $1; }
    ;



factor: '(' expr ')' { $$ = $2; }
      | NUMBER       { $$ = create_leaf($1); }
      ;
```

This grammar reflects the typical precedence of arithmetic operations—multiplication and division bind more tightly than addition and subtraction. The recursive structure of the rules naturally handles nested expressions, ensuring that the grouping of sub-expressions is maintained.

Semantic Translation of Arithmetic Expressions

When parsing arithmetic expressions, the semantic actions attached to each rule play a vital role. These actions are responsible for computing the result of the expression or constructing an AST that represents the arithmetic operations. For example, the action for the rule expr: expr '+' term might look like:

```
{ $$ = create_node("+", $1, $3); }
```

Here, the semantic action creates an AST node for the addition operator, linking the left-hand side expression and the term as child nodes. This action not only builds the tree structure but also encapsulates the arithmetic operation, which can later be evaluated or translated into code.

Handling Operator Overloading and Ambiguities

In some cases, arithmetic operators might be overloaded or have multiple meanings depending on context. YACC supports this by allowing the same operator symbol to be associated with different tokens or semantic actions. For example, the minus sign (−) can denote both binary subtraction and unary negation. To handle this, you can define separate grammar rules:

```
expr: '-' factor { $$ = create_node("NEG", NULL, $2); }
    | expr '-' term { $$ = create_node("-", $1, $3); }
    | term { $$ = $1; }
    ;
```

This approach distinguishes between the unary and binary uses of the operator, ensuring that each case is handled appropriately during translation. The semantic action for the unary minus creates a special node (perhaps with a label like "NEG") that signifies the negation of the factor.

Evaluating Arithmetic Expressions

Another approach to syntax-directed translation is to directly evaluate arithmetic expressions as they are parsed. This technique is useful in interpreters or simple calculators. In such cases, the semantic actions perform the actual arithmetic computation rather than building an AST. For example:

```
expr: expr '+' term { $$ = $1 + $3; }
   | expr '-' term { $$ = $1 - $3; }
   | term { $$ = $1; }
   ;


term: term '*' factor { $$ = $1 * $3; }
   | term '/' factor {
       if($3 == 0) {
          yyerror("Division by zero");
          $$ = 0;
       } else {
          $$ = $1 / $3;
       }
   }
   | factor { $$ = $1; }
   ;


factor: '(' expr ')' { $$ = $2; }
   | NUMBER { $$ = $1; }
   ;
```

In this scenario, the semantic actions use the arithmetic operators provided by the C language to compute the results. Although this approach sacrifices the creation of an intermediate representation, it is straightforward and efficient for many applications.

Combining Evaluation and AST Construction

Advanced translators often need to perform both immediate evaluation and build an AST for further processing. This can be achieved by designing semantic actions that simultaneously compute a value and construct a node. For instance, you might have an AST node that carries both the computed result and the operator information:

```
typedef struct {
   int value;
   ASTNode *node;
} EvalResult;
```

Then, your semantic actions can populate both fields:

```
expr: expr '+' term {
    EvalResult *res = malloc(sizeof(EvalResult));
    res->value = $1->value + $3->value;
    res->node = create_node("+", $1->node, $3->node);
    $$ = res;
  }
  | term { $$ = $1; }
  ;
```

This dual approach provides flexibility in scenarios where later compiler stages might need to perform optimizations based on the computed values or transform the AST for code generation.

Debugging and Validating Arithmetic Expressions

Given the complexity of arithmetic expressions, it is important to have robust debugging techniques. YACC's built-in debugging options, such as enabling yydebug, can help you trace the parsing process. Additionally, embedding print statements or logging within semantic actions can provide insights into how expressions are being reduced and how the AST is being constructed.

For instance, you might add logging to your semantic actions:

```
expr: expr '+' term {
    printf("Reducing: expr '+' term\n");
    $$ = create_node("+", $1, $3);
  }
  | term { $$ = $1; }
  ;
```

These debugging statements are invaluable during development and testing, as they allow you to verify that the grammar and semantic actions are working as intended.

5.4 Using YYSTYPE for Custom Data Types

Overview of Semantic Value Types

In YACC, every token and non-terminal symbol is associated with a semantic value. By default, YACC assumes these values are simple integers, but real-world applications often require more sophisticated data types. This is where YYSTYPE comes into play—a user-defined type that encapsulates the semantic information needed for syntax-directed translation. Customizing YYSTYPE is essential when building ASTs, performing type checking, or handling multiple data types in a language.

Defining a Custom YYSTYPE

To handle complex semantic values, you can redefine YYSTYPE as a union or structure that can represent various types of data. For instance, if your language supports both numeric expressions and string identifiers, you might define YYSTYPE as follows:

```
typedef union {
    int intval;
    char *strval;
    ASTNode *node;
} YYSTYPE;
```

This definition allows tokens to carry an integer, a string, or a pointer to an AST node, depending on the context. After defining YYSTYPE, you must inform YACC about the new type by including the definition in the definitions section of your grammar file, often within a %{ ... %} block.

Integrating YYSTYPE into Semantic Actions

Once YYSTYPE is defined, semantic actions in your grammar rules can use the custom fields to store and manipulate data. For example, consider the following semantic action in a rule for numeric expressions:

```
factor: NUMBER {
    $$ = malloc(sizeof(ASTNode));
    $$->type = NODE_NUMBER;
    $$->number = $1;
}
```

In this case, the semantic action allocates a new AST node, sets its type to represent a numeric literal, and assigns the numeric value from the token. With a custom YYSTYPE, the same token could also be used to store a string identifier or even a more complex data structure.

Managing Memory and Data Consistency

When using custom data types in YYSTYPE, memory management becomes a critical concern. Since semantic actions often involve dynamic memory allocation (e.g., when building AST nodes), you must ensure that allocated memory is properly deallocated at the appropriate time. Failure to manage memory correctly can lead to leaks or segmentation faults. A common strategy is to implement helper functions that both create and free the custom data types, ensuring that every allocation has a corresponding deallocation.

For example, if you create an AST node using create_node, you might also define a function free_node that recursively frees the memory associated with that node and its children. Ensuring consistency between allocation and deallocation is essential for building robust parsers, especially in long-running applications or those that process large volumes of data.

Example: Combining Multiple Data Types

Let's consider a scenario where you have both arithmetic expressions and variable assignments in your language. A custom YYSTYPE might be defined to support these constructs:

```c
typedef union {
    int intval;
    char *id;
    ASTNode *node;
} YYSTYPE;
```

With this definition, a token for a number would set intval, while an identifier token would set id. In your semantic actions, you can then inspect and use the appropriate field based on the context:

```c
assignment: IDENTIFIER '=' expr {
    ASTNode *assignNode = create_assignment_node($1, $3);
    $$ = assignNode;
}
;
```

Here, $1 might come from a token where YYSTYPE's id field is populated, and $3 would be an AST node resulting from the expression. This flexibility is crucial in languages with varied syntactic constructs.

Debugging Custom Data Types

When working with custom YYSTYPE definitions, debugging can be challenging due to the complexity of the data involved. One effective technique is to use logging or printing functions to display the contents of semantic values during parsing. This might involve writing a helper function that prints the contents of an AST node or a union variable, making it easier to trace the transformation of input into semantic representations.

For example:

```c
void print_ast(ASTNode *node) {
    if (!node) return;
    switch (node->type) {
        case NODE_NUMBER:
            printf("Number: %d\n", node->number);
            break;
```

```
        case NODE_OPERATOR:
            printf("Operator: %s\n", node->value);
            print_ast(node->left);
            print_ast(node->right);
            break;
        // Additional cases for other node types
    }
}
```

Integrating such debugging functions into your development process can help catch errors early and ensure that your custom YYSTYPE is being used correctly.

Extending YYSTYPE for Complex Languages

In more advanced compilers, the semantic value might need to represent even more complex data structures, such as symbol table entries, type information, or even intermediate representations for code generation. In these cases, YYSTYPE might be extended as follows:

```
typedef struct {
    ASTNode *ast;
    SymbolTableEntry *symbol;
    TypeInfo *type;
} SemanticValue;


typedef union {
    int intval;
    char *str;
    SemanticValue semVal;
} YYSTYPE;
```

This extended definition allows the parser to carry along rich semantic information at each step of the translation process. The semantic actions can then extract and manipulate these fields as needed, enabling sophisticated language processing techniques such as type inference and optimization.

5.5 Handling Errors in YACC

The Role of Error Handling in Translation

No parser is complete without robust error handling. In the context of syntax-directed translation, error handling is not merely about rejecting invalid input—it's about gracefully recovering from mistakes, providing meaningful error messages, and, when possible, continuing to parse the rest of the input. YACC provides built-in mechanisms to detect and recover from errors, allowing your syntax-directed translation system to be both user-friendly and resilient.

Strategies for Error Detection

YACC automatically invokes an error-handling function (typically named `yyerror()`) when it encounters syntax that does not match any valid production rule. It is crucial to implement this function so that it not only reports the error but also provides useful context, such as the line number or the nature of the error. A typical implementation might look like this:

```c
void yyerror(const char *s) {
    fprintf(stderr, "Syntax error at line %d: %s\n", yylineno, s);
}
```

This basic error-reporting mechanism can be enhanced with additional context, such as the unexpected token or the state of the parser when the error occurred.

Error Recovery Techniques

While error detection is the first step, error recovery is the next critical component. YACC supports error recovery by allowing you to specify the special token `error` within your grammar rules. This token can be used to indicate places where the parser should attempt to recover and continue parsing after an error is encountered. For example:

```
statement: error ';' { yyerror("Skipping invalid statement"); }
    | valid_statement
    ;
```

In this example, when the parser encounters an error while processing a statement, it will discard input until it reaches a semicolon and then resume parsing. This technique helps ensure that a single syntax error does not cascade into multiple error messages and that the parser can still build a partial translation of the input.

Embedding Error Recovery in Semantic Actions

Error recovery is not solely handled by the placement of the `error` token in the grammar. Semantic actions can also play a role in managing errors. For instance, if a semantic action detects an inconsistency (such as a type mismatch or an undefined variable), it can invoke `yyerror()` and either modify the AST or return a default value to allow parsing to continue. This approach allows for fine-grained control over error handling and can be tailored to the specific needs of your language.

Consider the following semantic action for an assignment statement that includes error recovery for type mismatches:

```
assignment: IDENTIFIER '=' expr {
    if (!check_type($1, $3)) {
        yyerror("Type mismatch in assignment");
        $$ = create_error_node("type_error");
    } else {
        $$ = create_assignment_node($1, $3);
    }
}
;
```

Here, instead of halting the parsing process entirely, the semantic action creates an error node in the AST. This node can later be used to generate a comprehensive error report or to enable further analysis despite the error.

Propagating and Reporting Errors

Effective error handling involves not only detecting and recovering from errors but also propagating them to later stages of compilation. When building an AST or generating intermediate code, it is important to mark nodes that were created as a result of error recovery. This marking enables later phases—such as semantic analysis or code generation—to treat these nodes differently, perhaps by skipping optimization on erroneous constructs or by generating specific error messages.

For example, an AST node might include an error flag:

```
typedef struct ast_node {
    NodeType type;
    char *value;
    int number;
    struct ast_node *left;
    struct ast_node *right;
    int error;  // 0 for no error, 1 for error detected
} ASTNode;
```

In your semantic actions, you can then set this flag when an error is encountered:

```
expr: expr '+' term {
    if ($1->error || $3->error) {
        $$ = create_error_node("error in addition");
        $$->error = 1;
    } else {
        $$ = create_node("+", $1, $3);
    }
}
;
```

This method allows the error information to be carried throughout the translation process, ensuring that any subsequent phases are aware of the problems detected during parsing.

Integrating Error Recovery with Debugging

Error recovery mechanisms are especially important during the development and debugging phases. YACC provides a debugging mode that can be enabled by setting the yydebug variable, which prints detailed information about parser states and token handling. Coupled with robust error messages, this debugging information can be used to pinpoint the location and nature of syntax errors more accurately.

Developers are encouraged to write comprehensive test cases that deliberately include syntax errors. These tests help ensure that the error recovery routines are effective and that the parser can continue processing despite encountering invalid input. For instance, a test suite might include malformed statements that trigger the error token, verifying that the parser skips to the appropriate recovery point without generating a cascade of error messages.

Advanced Error Recovery Techniques

In some sophisticated compilers, error recovery is not a simple matter of skipping tokens. Instead, the parser might attempt to insert missing tokens, perform local corrections, or even suggest possible fixes. While these advanced techniques can be complex to implement, YACC's flexibility allows developers to incorporate them within semantic actions. One approach is to maintain a lookahead buffer and, upon encountering an error, examine subsequent tokens to determine whether a particular correction might enable the parser to continue.

For example, if the parser expects a semicolon but encounters a different token, the semantic action might decide to insert a semicolon automatically, log a warning, and then proceed with parsing. Although such strategies can make the parser more forgiving, they must be used judiciously to avoid masking serious errors in the source code.

Best Practices for Error Handling

To summarize the best practices for error handling in YACC:

- **Clear Error Reporting:** Ensure that yyerror() provides meaningful information, including line numbers and context.
- **Strategic Use of the error Token:** Incorporate the error token in key places within your grammar to facilitate recovery without overwhelming the user with cascading errors.
- **Semantic Action Checks:** Embed error checks within semantic actions to catch semantic anomalies (such as type mismatches) early.
- **Error Propagation:** Mark error nodes in the AST to inform later compiler stages about problematic constructs.

- **Thorough Testing:** Use a comprehensive set of test cases to validate that error recovery works as expected and that the parser continues to operate in the presence of errors.
- **Balance Recovery and Strictness:** While it is useful to allow the parser to continue after encountering an error, ensure that recovery does not lead to misleading or ambiguous interpretations of the source code.

Chapter 6: Combining FLEX and YACC

Modern compiler construction often relies on a modular design, separating the concerns of lexical analysis and parsing. FLEX and YACC are two tools that, when used together, offer a powerful, flexible solution for language processing. While FLEX focuses on scanning the input and breaking it into tokens, YACC uses those tokens to construct a syntactic structure and drive semantic actions. This chapter details the process of combining these tools into a cohesive system, covering every aspect of integration from setup and communication to advanced symbol management and debugging.

6.1 The Rationale Behind Combining FLEX and YACC

Overview of the Integration Philosophy

Combining FLEX and YACC is a tried-and-true approach that has influenced compiler construction for decades. The rationale behind this combination lies in the clear separation of concerns:

- **Lexical Analysis (FLEX):** The lexer reads the raw input, recognizes patterns defined by regular expressions, and groups characters into tokens. This module is designed to be fast and efficient.
- **Syntactic Parsing (YACC):** Once tokens are produced, the parser organizes them according to the language's grammar, building a syntactic structure (such as a parse tree or an abstract syntax tree) and triggering semantic actions as it recognizes language constructs.

This modular design allows developers to focus on language-specific rules in each phase without getting bogged down by details that belong to the other phase. By combining FLEX and YACC, you create a pipeline where each tool performs its specialized role, resulting in a system that is easier to maintain, test, and extend.

Benefits of a Modular Approach

The separation of lexical analysis from parsing offers several key benefits:

- **Maintainability:** Changes in the lexical rules (such as adding a new keyword) can be handled in the FLEX file without affecting the grammar in YACC. Similarly, modifications to grammar rules do not require adjustments to the lexer.
- **Debugging Ease:** With clearly delineated responsibilities, debugging becomes simpler. You can isolate problems to either the lexer or the parser.
- **Reusability:** A well-written lexer can be reused in different parsing contexts. Similarly, grammar rules defined in YACC can be adapted to similar languages with minor changes.
- **Scalability:** As languages grow in complexity, a modular approach ensures that each component can be optimized individually. For example, performance tuning of the lexer can be done without interfering with the parser's structure.

Historical Context and Modern Relevance

The combined use of FLEX and YACC originated in the early days of Unix and continues to be relevant today. Although modern alternatives exist (such as ANTLR or Bison), the FLEX–YACC combination remains popular in educational settings and for building lightweight compilers or interpreters for domain-specific languages. The principles behind their integration—separation of concerns, modularity, and robust error handling—continue to be applicable in modern language processing frameworks.

6.2 Setting Up the Integrated Environment

Preparing Your Development Environment

Before integrating FLEX and YACC, it is essential to set up an environment where both tools can operate seamlessly. This typically involves installing the tools on your system, configuring your build environment, and creating a project structure that clearly separates lexical, syntactic, and support code.

Installation

Most Unix-like systems include FLEX and YACC (or a compatible variant such as Bison) in their package repositories. On a Linux system, you might install them with commands like:

```
sudo apt-get install flex bison
```

For other systems, similar package management commands apply. Ensure that your compiler (such as GCC) is available, as both FLEX and YACC output C source code.

Directory Structure

A well-organized project might have a directory structure such as:

```
project_root/
├── src/
│    ├── lexer.l        # FLEX source file
│    ├── parser.y       # YACC source file
│    ├── common.h       # Common header file for shared definitions
│    └── main.c         # Main function to start the parser
├── build/              # Build output (object files, executables)
└── Makefile            # Automated build instructions
```

This structure ensures that lexical definitions, grammar rules, and support code are clearly separated and that shared definitions (such as token constants) are placed in a common header file.

Creating a Makefile for Automation

Automating the build process using a Makefile is a best practice when combining FLEX and YACC. A typical Makefile might include rules that regenerate source files whenever the lexer or parser definitions change. An example Makefile is shown below:

```
# Define the target executable
TARGET = mycompiler


# Define source files
YACC_SRC = src/parser.y
FLEX_SRC = src/lexer.l
MAIN_SRC = src/main.c


# Define generated files
YACC_C = build/y.tab.c
YACC_H = build/y.tab.h
FLEX_C = build/lex.yy.c


# Compiler settings
CC = gcc
CFLAGS = -g -Wall -Ibuild
LDFLAGS = -ll


all: $(TARGET)
```

```
$(YACC_C) $(YACC_H): $(YACC_SRC)
        @mkdir -p build
        bison -d -o $(YACC_C) $(YACC_SRC)
        mv y.tab.h $(YACC_H)


$(FLEX_C): $(FLEX_SRC) $(YACC_H)
        @mkdir -p build
        flex -o $(FLEX_C) $(FLEX_SRC)


$(TARGET): $(YACC_C) $(FLEX_C) $(MAIN_SRC)
        $(CC) $(CFLAGS) -o $(TARGET) $(YACC_C) $(FLEX_C) $(MAIN_SRC)
$(LDFLAGS)


clean:
        rm -rf build $(TARGET)
```

This Makefile includes targets for generating YACC output, compiling the FLEX file, and linking everything together with the main program. It also ensures that header files (such as y.tab.h) are placed in a directory that both the lexer and the main program can access.

Integrating Shared Definitions

A common issue when combining FLEX and YACC is ensuring that both tools share consistent definitions for tokens and other constants. This is typically managed by including a common header file. For example, the header file common.h might contain:

```
#ifndef COMMON_H
#define COMMON_H


/* Token definitions for use by both FLEX and YACC */
enum yytokentype {
    NUMBER = 258,
    IDENTIFIER,
    PLUS,
    MINUS,
    MULTIPLY,
    DIVIDE,
    LPAREN,
    RPAREN,
    SEMICOLON,
    ASSIGN,
    // Other tokens...
```

```
};

#endif /* COMMON_H */
```

Then, both the FLEX file (lexer.l) and the YACC file (parser.y) can include this header:

In lexer.l:

```
%{
#include "common.h"
%}
```

In parser.y:

```
%{
#include "common.h"
%}
```

This shared header ensures that both parts of the system agree on token codes and other definitions, avoiding mismatches that could lead to difficult-to-debug errors.

6.3 Communicating Between the Lexer and Parser

The Role of yylex()

The function yylex() is the bridge between FLEX and YACC. When YACC needs the next token, it calls yylex(), which is implemented by FLEX. This function scans the input stream, matches patterns based on regular expressions, and returns the corresponding token value to YACC.

Passing Tokens and Semantic Values

Each token returned by yylex() carries a semantic value that YACC uses in its grammar rules. These values are stored in the global variable yylval. For example, if a numeric literal is recognized, yylex() might convert the string to an integer and assign it to yylval:

```
%{
#include "common.h"
#include <stdlib.h>
%}
```

```
%%

[0-9]+  { yylval = atoi(yytext); return NUMBER; }
[a-zA-Z_][a-zA-Z0-9_]* { return IDENTIFIER; }
"+"     { return PLUS; }
"-"     { return MINUS; }
"*"     { return MULTIPLY; }
"/"     { return DIVIDE; }
"("     { return LPAREN; }
")"     { return RPAREN; }
";"     { return SEMICOLON; }
"="     { return ASSIGN; }
[ \t\n]+    ; /* Ignore whitespace */
.       { printf("Unexpected character: %s\n", yytext); }
%%


int yywrap(void) {
    return 1;
}
```

In this example, each rule matches a specific pattern and returns a token. The semantic value (for numbers) is assigned before returning the token. When YACC receives the token, it uses the value stored in yylval for further semantic actions. This mechanism is central to the cooperation between FLEX and YACC.

Token Precedence and Lexical Ambiguities

When the lexer and parser work together, it is important to handle lexical ambiguities. For instance, a word might serve as both an identifier and a reserved keyword. In the FLEX file, you can perform a lookup against a table of reserved words. If a match is found, return the reserved keyword's token; otherwise, return the generic identifier token. Consider the following code snippet:

```
%{
#include "common.h"
#include <string.h>
#include <stdlib.h>


typedef struct {
    const char *name;
    int token;
} ReservedWord;
```

```
ReservedWord reserved[] = {
    {"if", IF},
    {"else", ELSE},
    {"while", WHILE},
    {"return", RETURN},
    {NULL, 0}
};


int lookup_reserved(const char *str) {
    for (int i = 0; reserved[i].name != NULL; i++) {
        if (strcmp(str, reserved[i].name) == 0)
            return reserved[i].token;
    }
    return IDENTIFIER;
}
%}


[a-zA-Z_][a-zA-Z0-9_]* {
    int token = lookup_reserved(yytext);
    if (token == IDENTIFIER)
        yylval = strdup(yytext);  /* Allocate memory for identifier strings */
    return token;
}
```

This snippet demonstrates how the lexer checks for reserved keywords and assigns the correct token. By doing so, you ensure that the parser receives the appropriate tokens for language constructs.

Handling Complex Semantic Values

For languages with more complex semantics, the communication between the lexer and parser might involve passing structures or pointers rather than simple integers. This is where a customized YYSTYPE (as described in previous chapters) becomes essential. In the FLEX file, you would set yylval to point to a dynamically allocated structure containing all necessary information about the token. YACC's grammar rules then extract and use this information during semantic analysis.

Synchronization and Error Propagation

Errors in the lexer can impact the parser, so robust error handling and synchronization are necessary. If the lexer encounters an invalid token, it should report the error (using a function like yyerror()) and, when possible, recover by skipping characters until a recognizable pattern is found. The parser can also use special error tokens to synchronize and resume parsing. For example, when an unexpected token is

encountered, the parser may invoke an error recovery routine that calls yylex()
repeatedly until a semicolon or a known delimiter is found.

6.4 Advanced Symbol Table Management

The Importance of a Symbol Table

A symbol table is a central data structure in many language processors. It maintains a
record of identifiers, their types, scope information, and sometimes even memory
locations. In the combined FLEX and YACC environment, managing a symbol table is
critical to ensuring that both lexical analysis and parsing have access to consistent
information about the program's symbols.

Integrating Symbol Table Management

The lexer, when recognizing identifiers, often needs to consult the symbol table to
determine whether an identifier is a variable, a keyword, or a function name. Similarly,
the parser may need to insert new symbols during declaration processing or look up
symbols during semantic analysis. A common strategy is to implement the symbol table
as a separate module that both FLEX and YACC can call.

For instance, you might create a file named symtable.c with functions like
insert_symbol(), lookup_symbol(), and print_symbol_table(). A simple
implementation using a hash table might look like this:

```
#include <stdio.h>
#include <stdlib.h>
#include <string.h>
#include "symtable.h"


#define TABLE_SIZE 101


typedef struct Symbol {
    char *name;
    int type;
    struct Symbol *next;
} Symbol;


Symbol *table[TABLE_SIZE];


unsigned int hash(const char *s) {
    unsigned int hashval = 0;
    while (*s)
```

```
      hashval = (hashval << 5) + *s++;
    return hashval % TABLE_SIZE;
}


Symbol *lookup_symbol(const char *name) {
    unsigned int index = hash(name);
    Symbol *sym = table[index];
    while (sym != NULL) {
      if (strcmp(sym->name, name) == 0)
          return sym;
      sym = sym->next;
    }
    return NULL;
}


Symbol *insert_symbol(const char *name, int type) {
    unsigned int index = hash(name);
    Symbol *sym = lookup_symbol(name);
    if (sym == NULL) {
        sym = (Symbol *)malloc(sizeof(Symbol));
        sym->name = strdup(name);
        sym->type = type;
        sym->next = table[index];
        table[index] = sym;
    }
    return sym;
}


void print_symbol_table(void) {
    for (int i = 0; i < TABLE_SIZE; i++) {
        Symbol *sym = table[i];
        while (sym) {
            printf("Symbol: %s, Type: %d\n", sym->name, sym->type);
            sym = sym->next;
        }
    }
}
```

Using the Symbol Table in FLEX and YACC

In the FLEX file, when an identifier is recognized, you might call lookup_symbol () to check if the identifier already exists or insert_symbol () to add it if it is new. For example:

```
[a-zA-Z_][a-zA-Z0-9_]* {
    int token = lookup_reserved(yytext);
    if (token == IDENTIFIER) {
        Symbol *sym = lookup_symbol(yytext);
        if (sym == NULL) {
            sym = insert_symbol(yytext, /* appropriate type */ 0);
        }
        yylval = (int)sym; // Passing pointer as semantic value
    }
    return token;
}
```

In the YACC file, during declaration or assignment rules, the symbol table functions can be invoked to perform semantic checks. For instance, in an assignment statement rule, you might ensure that the identifier has been declared and has the correct type:

```
assignment:
    IDENTIFIER ASSIGN expr {
        Symbol *sym = (Symbol *)$1;
        if (sym == NULL) {
            yyerror("Undeclared identifier");
        } else {
            // Optionally check type compatibility and update symbol table
            printf("Assigning value to symbol %s\n", sym->name);
        }
    }
    ;
```

Managing Scope and Lifetime

For languages that support scoping, the symbol table module must be extended to handle nested scopes. One common approach is to implement the symbol table as a stack of hash tables—each representing a scope. When entering a new block, a new table is pushed onto the stack; when exiting, it is popped off. This design enables the lexer and parser to resolve identifiers according to the current scope. Techniques for scope management include:

- **Global vs. Local Scopes:** Differentiating between global declarations and those local to a function or block.
- **Block Scope:** Managing nested scopes by linking symbol table entries to their respective blocks.
- **Shadowing:** Allowing inner scopes to redefine identifiers without affecting the outer scopes.

Implementing scope management requires careful design, but it can be integrated seamlessly into the FLEX and YACC system by adding appropriate functions to the symbol table module (such as enter_scope() and exit_scope()).

Practical Considerations and Optimization

Symbol table management can have a significant impact on performance, especially for large programs. Techniques such as efficient hashing, memory pooling, and lazy insertion are common optimizations. Moreover, integrating the symbol table with debugging facilities—such as printing the table after parsing—can be very helpful during development.

6.5 Handling Reserved Keywords and Identifiers

Distinguishing Keywords from Identifiers

A key challenge for the lexer is to differentiate between reserved keywords and general identifiers. Keywords have a fixed meaning in the language (such as control-flow constructs or data types), while identifiers represent variable names, function names, etc. The FLEX file typically contains rules that check whether a matched pattern is a keyword by consulting a reserved word table.

Techniques for Keyword Recognition

Several techniques can be employed to handle reserved keywords:

Direct Pattern Matching: Define individual patterns for each reserved keyword. For example:

```
"if"     { return IF; }
"else"   { return ELSE; }
"while"  { return WHILE; }
```

1. This approach works well when the number of keywords is small and the performance impact is negligible.
2. **Lookup Tables:** As shown earlier, match a generic identifier pattern and then perform a lookup in an array or hash table of reserved words. This approach is more scalable for languages with many keywords.
3. **Hybrid Methods:** Use a combination of direct matching and lookups to optimize for common keywords while still handling less frequent ones efficiently.

Passing Keyword Information to YACC

When a keyword is recognized, the lexer returns a token corresponding to that keyword. In the YACC grammar, different keywords are then handled by distinct production rules. For example, a rule for an if statement might look like:

```
if_statement:
    IF '(' expr ')' statement { $$ = create_if_node($3, $5, NULL); }
    | IF '(' expr ')' statement ELSE statement { $$ = create_if_node($3, $5, $7); }
```

```
;
```

This clear separation ensures that keywords are processed with their intended semantics. The lexer must consistently return the correct token, which is why sharing a common header file (as described in Section 6.2) is critical.

Memory Management for Identifiers

When identifiers are not keywords, the lexer may allocate memory to store the string value. It is important to ensure that this memory is managed correctly to avoid leaks. Typically, once the identifier's semantic value is passed to the parser and possibly stored in the symbol table, the allocated memory should be freed when no longer needed. In practice, the symbol table module might take responsibility for the lifetime of identifier strings.

Integrating with Semantic Actions

Semantic actions in YACC can access the textual value of identifiers and keywords by using the appropriate fields in yylval (or a custom YYSTYPE). For instance, if an identifier token sets yylval to point to a dynamically allocated string, a semantic action might look like:

```
variable:
    IDENTIFIER { $$ = create_variable_node($1); free($1); }
;
```

Here, after creating the variable node, the semantic action frees the string. This careful management ensures that the integration between FLEX and YACC is both robust and efficient.

6.6 Debugging and Testing the Combined System

The Challenges of Integrated Debugging

When FLEX and YACC are combined, errors can originate in either module or in their interaction. Debugging such an integrated system requires strategies that span both lexical analysis and parsing. Common issues include mismatches in token definitions, incorrect semantic value propagation, and synchronization problems between the lexer and the parser.

Enabling Debugging in YACC

YACC offers built-in debugging support that can be enabled by setting the global variable yydebug. For example, adding the following code to your main function can produce detailed trace output:

```
#include <stdio.h>


int main(void) {
    yydebug = 1; // Enable YACC debugging
    yyparse();
    return 0;
}
```

This debugging output provides insight into the parser's state transitions, token consumption, and the application of semantic actions.

Debugging Techniques for FLEX

While FLEX does not have as extensive a debugging mode as YACC, you can embed print statements within the rules to log recognized patterns. For example:

```
[0-9]+ {
    printf("Lexed NUMBER: %s\n", yytext);
    yylval = atoi(yytext);
    return NUMBER;
}
```

These logs can help you trace how the input is tokenized and ensure that tokens are passed correctly to YACC.

Integrated Testing Strategies

For an integrated FLEX–YACC system, testing should be performed at multiple levels:

- **Unit Testing:** Test the lexer and parser separately using controlled inputs. For example, run the lexer on sample strings to verify that tokens are generated as expected.
- **Integration Testing:** Combine the lexer and parser and run end-to-end tests with a variety of inputs, including both valid and invalid code.
- **Regression Testing:** Maintain a suite of test cases that cover all language constructs. This is critical when making changes to the grammar or lexical rules to ensure that new modifications do not break existing functionality.

Common Pitfalls and Their Remedies

Some common issues encountered when combining FLEX and YACC include:

- **Token Mismatch:** If the lexer returns a token that YACC does not expect, errors occur. Ensure that token definitions in the common header file are identical in both modules.

- **Memory Leaks:** Dynamic memory allocation in the lexer or semantic actions must be managed carefully. Use tools such as Valgrind to check for leaks.
- **Synchronization Errors:** When error recovery is implemented, the lexer and parser must synchronize correctly. Debug traces can help pinpoint where synchronization fails, and strategic use of the error token in YACC can improve recovery.
- **Scope and Lifetime Issues:** When passing pointers (for identifiers or AST nodes), ensure that the lifetime of the data is appropriate. This is especially important when using a symbol table that manages memory.

Advanced Debugging Tools

For large projects, consider integrating advanced debugging tools such as:

- **GDB:** The GNU Debugger can be used to step through both the lexer and parser code. Set breakpoints in yylex(), semantic actions, or symbol table functions to trace the execution.
- **Logging Libraries:** Instead of using printf(), you might incorporate a logging library that allows for different log levels (debug, info, warning, error). This approach makes it easier to disable verbose logging in production builds.

6.7 Case Studies and Practical Examples

A Simple Calculator Revisited

One of the most common examples of integrating FLEX and YACC is the simple calculator. In this example, the lexer identifies numeric literals, arithmetic operators, and parentheses, while the parser builds an AST and computes the result.

Example FLEX File (lexer.l)

```
%{
#include "common.h"
#include <stdlib.h>
#include <stdio.h>
%}


%%


[0-9]+ {
    printf("Lexed NUMBER: %s\n", yytext);
    yylval = atoi(yytext);
    return NUMBER;
}
"("    { return LPAREN; }
")"    { return RPAREN; }
```

```
"+"    { return PLUS; }
"-"    { return MINUS; }
"*"    { return MULTIPLY; }
"/"    { return DIVIDE; }
[ \t\n]+   ;  /* Skip whitespace */
.      { printf("Unknown character: %s\n", yytext); }
%%


int yywrap(void) {
    return 1;
}
```

Example YACC File (parser.y)

```
%{
#include <stdio.h>
#include <stdlib.h>
#include "common.h"
void yyerror(const char *s);
%}


%token NUMBER LPAREN RPAREN PLUS MINUS MULTIPLY DIVIDE
%left '+' '-'
%left '*' '/'


%%
expr: expr PLUS expr { $$ = $1 + $3; }
   | expr MINUS expr { $$ = $1 - $3; }
   | expr MULTIPLY expr { $$ = $1 * $3; }
   | expr DIVIDE expr {
       if($3 == 0) {
           yyerror("Division by zero");
           $$ = 0;
       } else {
           $$ = $1 / $3;
       }
    }
   | LPAREN expr RPAREN { $$ = $2; }
   | NUMBER { $$ = $1; }
   ;
%%


void yyerror(const char *s) {
    fprintf(stderr, "Error: %s\n", s);
```

```
}

int main(void) {
    printf("Enter an expression: ");
    yyparse();
    return 0;
}
```

In this example, the calculator uses FLEX to tokenize the input and YACC to parse the expression. The integration is seamless, with token definitions shared via the header file and the two modules linked together during compilation.

A Mini Programming Language

For a more advanced example, consider a mini programming language that supports variable declarations, assignments, and simple control structures. In this system, the lexer must recognize identifiers and reserved keywords, while the parser builds an AST and integrates with a symbol table.

Symbol Table Integration

Suppose you have a symbol table module (symtable.c and symtable.h) as described earlier. The lexer, upon encountering an identifier, checks the symbol table and returns a pointer in yylval. The parser then uses this information to construct semantic nodes representing variable declarations and assignments.

Example Integration in the Lexer

```
%{
#include "common.h"
#include "symtable.h"
#include <string.h>
%}


%%


[a-zA-Z_][a-zA-Z0-9_]* {
    int token = lookup_reserved(yytext);
    if (token == IDENTIFIER) {
        Symbol *sym = lookup_symbol(yytext);
        if (sym == NULL)
            sym = insert_symbol(yytext, 0); // Type information would be set later
        yylval = (int)sym;
    }
```

```
    return token;
}
```

Example Parser Rule for Variable Declaration

```
declaration:
    IDENTIFIER {
        Symbol *sym = (Symbol *)$1;
        printf("Declared variable: %s\n", sym->name);
        $$ = create_declaration_node(sym);
    }
    ;
```

This mini language example demonstrates a more realistic scenario where combining FLEX and YACC enables the creation of a full compiler front-end that processes declarations, statements, and expressions in a unified manner.

6.8 Best Practices and Performance Optimization

Modular Design and Code Organization

When integrating FLEX and YACC, organizing your code into logical modules is key to maintainability. Keep lexical rules, grammar rules, symbol table management, and utility functions in separate files. Use common header files to share definitions, and document your code thoroughly so that the interactions between modules are clear.

Optimizing the Lexer

The performance of the lexer can be crucial in a language processing system. To optimize your FLEX file:

- **Use Efficient Regular Expressions:** Write patterns that minimize backtracking and avoid ambiguous matches.
- **Minimize Actions:** Keep the code in actions short, delegating complex logic to functions defined in separate files.
- **Buffering:** Consider using input buffering techniques if processing very large files.

Optimizing the Parser

The YACC-generated parser can be optimized by:

- **Refining Grammar Rules:** Simplify grammar rules to reduce conflicts and improve parse table efficiency.
- **Reducing Semantic Action Overhead:** Delegate heavy computations to external functions and keep inline actions minimal.

- **Debugging Options:** Disable debugging output (e.g., setting yydebug to 0) in production builds to enhance performance.

Memory Management

Memory allocation and deallocation must be carefully managed, especially when constructing ASTs and managing symbol tables. Use memory pools or garbage collection techniques where appropriate, and always pair allocations with corresponding frees. Tools like Valgrind can help you detect memory leaks early in development.

Profiling and Benchmarking

Profiling the integrated system can identify bottlenecks in both lexical analysis and parsing. Use profiling tools (such as gprof or perf) to analyze CPU usage and optimize critical sections of code. Regularly benchmark your system with realistic inputs to ensure that performance improvements are maintained as the language features expand.

Chapter 7: Intermediate and Advanced Parsing Techniques

Parsing is a central phase in language processing that takes the token stream produced by lexical analysis and organizes it into a structured, hierarchical representation of the source program. While the fundamentals of parsing may seem straightforward when dealing with well-behaved grammars, real-world languages are rarely so simple. In this chapter, we address the challenges encountered when grammars exhibit ambiguities, non-trivial recursive structures, nested constructs, and other complexities. We also explore strategies to enhance the robustness and flexibility of your parsers, especially when using YACC (or similar parser generators).

Parsing advanced language constructs requires a combination of theoretical insights and practical techniques. Throughout this chapter, we will not only discuss the underlying concepts but also illustrate them with code examples and detailed explanations of how each technique can be implemented. The aim is to provide you with a toolkit of intermediate and advanced parsing techniques that can be applied to build compilers, interpreters, or any system that requires sophisticated language processing.

7.1 Ambiguities in Grammar and How to Resolve Them

Understanding Grammar Ambiguity

In formal language theory, a grammar is considered ambiguous if a particular string can be generated by the grammar in more than one way. Ambiguity is a significant issue because it means that the parse tree—the structure that represents the syntactic structure of the input—is not unique. For a compiler, this could lead to inconsistent interpretations of the source code. Ambiguity is common in natural language and, unfortunately, in programming languages when the grammar is not carefully designed.

For example, consider a simplified grammar for arithmetic expressions:

```
Expr → Expr '+' Expr
  | Expr '*' Expr
  | '(' Expr ')'
  | NUMBER
```

In this grammar, the expression

```
3 + 4 * 5
```

could be parsed as either

```
(3+4)*5(3 + 4) * 5 or


3+(4*5)3 + (4 * 5)
```

Without additional information, the parser does not know which interpretation is intended. Resolving this ambiguity is crucial to ensure that the parsed structure accurately reflects the intended meaning of the input.

Techniques to Resolve Ambiguity

There are several techniques to resolve ambiguities in grammars:

1.   **Operator Precedence and Associativity:** One common method, particularly for arithmetic expressions, is to define operator precedence and associativity rules. By specifying that multiplication has higher precedence than addition (and that addition is left-associative), you force the grammar to resolve the ambiguity in favor of the intended interpretation. In YACC, this is typically done using directives such as %left and %right.

2.   **Grammar Refactoring:** Sometimes, you can rewrite the grammar to remove ambiguity altogether. This involves restructuring the production rules so that every valid input has a unique parse tree. For arithmetic expressions, a typical refactoring might separate the grammar into different non-terminals for each level of precedence:

```
expr: term
  | expr '+' term
  | expr '-' term
  ;


term: factor
  | term '*' factor
```

```
    | term '/' factor
    ;


factor: '(' expr ')'
    | NUMBER
    ;
```

This decomposition makes the precedence explicit in the structure of the grammar.

3.   **Semantic Actions to Guide Disambiguation:** In some cases, ambiguities cannot be entirely resolved by grammar restructuring alone. Instead, you can incorporate semantic actions that use additional context or runtime information to choose between ambiguous alternatives. For instance, when dealing with overloaded operators or context-sensitive constructs, the semantic action might inspect the types or values involved to decide the correct parse tree.

4.   **Precedence Declarations in YACC:** YACC provides a built-in mechanism to resolve shift/reduce conflicts arising from ambiguous grammar. You can declare precedence and associativity for tokens, and YACC uses this information to decide whether to shift (read another token) or reduce (apply a grammar rule) when a conflict occurs. For example:

```
%left '+' '-'
%left '*' '/'
```

These declarations inform YACC that $*$ and $/$ have higher precedence than $+$ and $-$, and that the operators are left-associative. This greatly reduces the potential for ambiguity in arithmetic expressions.

Examples and Practical Considerations

Let's take a detailed look at an example that demonstrates resolving ambiguity using precedence rules. Consider a fragment of a YACC file designed to parse arithmetic expressions:

```
%{
#include <stdio.h>
#include <stdlib.h>
void yyerror(const char *s);
%}


%token NUMBER
%left '+' '-'
%left '*' '/'
```

```
%%
expr: expr '+' expr { $$ = $1 + $3; }
    | expr '-' expr { $$ = $1 - $3; }
    | expr '*' expr { $$ = $1 * $3; }
    | expr '/' expr {
        if ($3 == 0) {
            yyerror("Division by zero");
            $$ = 0;
        } else {
            $$ = $1 / $3;
        }
    }
    | '(' expr ')'  { $$ = $2; }
    | NUMBER        { $$ = $1; }
    ;
%%
```

In this example, the precedence declarations ensure that when the input "3 + 4 * 5" is parsed, the multiplication is performed before the addition. Without these declarations, the grammar would be ambiguous, and the generated parser might produce unexpected results.

Advanced Ambiguity Resolution

Beyond operator precedence, other forms of ambiguity can arise in language constructs such as conditional statements, loops, and even function definitions. A classic example is the "dangling else" problem, where it is ambiguous to which if statement an else clause belongs. Consider the following grammar:

```
stmt: IF '(' expr ')' stmt
    | IF '(' expr ')' stmt ELSE stmt
    | other
    ;
```

The ambiguity here is that in a nested if statement without explicit braces, it is unclear whether an else belongs to the inner or outer if. To resolve this, the grammar can be refactored into two non-terminals: one for statements that may have an unmatched if and one for those that are complete. For example:

```
stmt: matched_stmt
    | unmatched_stmt
    ;
```

```
matched_stmt:
    IF '(' expr ')' matched_stmt ELSE matched_stmt
    | other
    ;


unmatched_stmt:
    IF '(' expr ')' stmt
    | IF '(' expr ')' matched_stmt ELSE unmatched_stmt
    ;
```

This approach forces the parser to correctly match each else with its intended if, eliminating the ambiguity.

7.2 Left Recursion and Right Recursion

The Concept of Recursion in Grammars

Recursion in grammar production rules is a powerful mechanism that allows languages to describe infinitely large constructs with a finite set of rules. There are two primary forms of recursion: left recursion and right recursion. The choice between these forms has significant implications for how parsers, particularly bottom-up parsers like those generated by YACC, operate.

Left Recursion: A production is left-recursive if the non-terminal appears as the leftmost symbol on the right-hand side of a rule. For example:

```
Expr → Expr '+' Term | Term
```

Here, Expr calls itself on the left side, making it left-recursive. Left recursion is natural for representing left-associative operations but can cause issues with certain parsing algorithms.

Right Recursion: Conversely, a production is right-recursive if the non-terminal appears as the rightmost symbol on the right-hand side:

```
Expr → Term | Term '+' Expr
```

Right recursion is often used to represent right-associative constructs and tends to be more suitable for top-down parsers.

Implications for Bottom-Up Parsing

Bottom-up parsers such as those generated by YACC are generally well-equipped to handle left recursion. In fact, left recursion is preferred in these cases because it naturally supports left-associative operators. However, excessive left recursion can sometimes lead to large parse tables or performance issues if not managed properly. Right recursion, while more natural for top-down parsers, can also be used in bottom-up parsing; however, it may require additional rules or actions to enforce associativity.

Converting Between Left and Right Recursion

In some scenarios, you might need to convert a left-recursive grammar to a right-recursive one or vice versa to meet the needs of a particular parsing strategy. This conversion involves reworking the grammar rules while preserving the language they generate.

For example, consider a left-recursive rule for a list of items:

```
list: list ',' item
  | item
  ;
```

This can be converted to a right-recursive form by rewriting it as:

```
list: item list_tail
  ;


list_tail: ',' item list_tail
     | /* empty */
     ;
```

This transformation makes the recursion right-associated, which can sometimes simplify certain parsing tasks or improve error recovery in a top-down parsing context.

Semantic Considerations in Recursive Rules

When implementing semantic actions for recursive rules, you must carefully manage how the parse tree is built and how semantic values are propagated. In a left-recursive grammar, the semantic actions tend to combine the left-hand side values before processing the right-hand side. For instance, in an arithmetic expression:

```
expr: expr '+' term { $$ = create_node("+", $1, $3); }
  | term { $$ = $1; }
```

```
;
```

The left recursion ensures that the left-hand side of the expression is built first, which is ideal for left-associative operations like addition and subtraction. When converting to right recursion, the semantic actions must be adapted accordingly. The choice of recursion form will directly influence the shape of the abstract syntax tree (AST) and how operations are grouped.

Practical Example: Expression Parsing

Let's consider a practical example that demonstrates both left and right recursion in the context of arithmetic expressions.

Left-Recursive Example

```
expr: expr '+' term { $$ = create_node("+", $1, $3); }
   | expr '-' term { $$ = create_node("-", $1, $3); }
   | term { $$ = $1; }
   ;


term: term '*' factor { $$ = create_node("*", $1, $3); }
   | term '/' factor { $$ = create_node("/", $1, $3); }
   | factor { $$ = $1; }
   ;


factor: '(' expr ')' { $$ = $2; }
    | NUMBER { $$ = create_leaf($1); }
    ;
```

In this left-recursive design, each recursive call builds on the result of the previous one. This is a natural representation for left-associative operations where, for example, "a – b – c" is interpreted as (a–b)–c(a – b) – c.

Right-Recursive Example

An equivalent right-recursive grammar might look like this:

```
expr: term expr_tail { $$ = $2 ? create_node($2->op, $1, $2->node) : $1; }
   ;


expr_tail: '+' term expr_tail {
        ASTNode *node = create_node("+", $2, $3 ? $3->node : NULL);
        $$ = create_tail(node);
    }
```

```
        | '-' term expr_tail {
            ASTNode *node = create_node("-", $2, $3 ? $3->node : NULL);
            $$ = create_tail(node);
        }
        | /* empty */ { $$ = NULL; }
        ;
```

In this right-recursive version, the tail of the expression is built separately and then combined with the term. Although this form can be less intuitive for left-associative operations, it is useful when a top-down parser is employed or when specific semantic processing requires a right-associated structure.

Comparing Performance and Clarity

From a performance standpoint, left recursion is typically more efficient for bottom-up parsers like YACC. However, the choice between left and right recursion should be made based on the desired semantic structure and the clarity of the grammar. For example, when designing a language with both left- and right-associative operators, you may need to mix both forms in a way that accurately reflects the language semantics.

7.3 Handling Nested Structures (Expressions, Blocks)

The Challenge of Nested Constructs

Modern programming languages often allow for deeply nested constructs such as expressions, code blocks, loops, and conditional statements. Handling these nested structures correctly is critical for any parser, as mistakes can lead to misinterpretation of the input and faulty program behavior. Nested constructs increase the complexity of the grammar and the corresponding semantic actions, necessitating sophisticated parsing techniques.

Representing Nesting in Grammar

The most straightforward way to represent nested constructs is through recursive grammar rules. For example, to handle nested parentheses in arithmetic expressions, you might define a rule like:

```
factor: '(' expr ')' { $$ = $2; }
    | NUMBER { $$ = create_leaf($1); }
    ;
```

This rule allows an expression to be nested arbitrarily deep by recursively invoking expr within parentheses. For nested blocks (such as those found in C-like languages), the grammar might include rules for compound statements:

```
compound_stmt: '{' stmt_list '}' { $$ = create_compound_node($2); }
    ;


stmt_list: stmt_list stmt { $$ = append_statement($1, $2); }
    | stmt { $$ = create_statement_list($1); }
    ;
```

This design allows blocks to be nested within one another without limitation.

Semantic Actions for Nested Structures

When dealing with nested structures, semantic actions play a critical role in constructing the parse tree and ensuring that each nested level is correctly represented. For instance, when parsing a compound statement, the semantic action should build a node that contains a list of child statements, each of which may be a simple statement or another compound statement.

Consider the following example of a semantic action for a compound statement:

```
compound_stmt: '{' stmt_list '}' {
    $$ = create_compound_node($2);
}
    ;
```

In this example, `create_compound_node()` is a function that creates an AST node representing the block. The function takes the list of statements produced by `stmt_list` and constructs a node that encapsulates all the nested information. This approach ensures that later stages of the compiler can process nested blocks uniformly, regardless of their depth.

Managing Deep Nesting

One challenge with nested constructs is the potential for deep recursion, which can strain both the parser's stack and the efficiency of semantic actions. To manage deep nesting, several strategies may be employed:

- **Tail Recursion Optimization:** In some cases, grammars can be written to use tail recursion, which is more amenable to optimization by the compiler. This can reduce the overhead associated with deeply nested structures.
- **Iterative Constructs:** Where possible, iterative solutions (such as loops) can be used in semantic actions to construct lists or trees, reducing the reliance on recursive function calls.
- **Stack-Based Parsing Techniques:** Some parsing algorithms use an explicit stack to manage nested structures rather than relying solely on the call stack. This approach can provide greater control over memory usage and error recovery in deeply nested contexts.

Handling Nested Expressions

Nested expressions, such as those found in mathematical formulas or complex logical conditions, are a frequent source of challenges in parsing. The key is to ensure that every opening delimiter (like '(' or '{') is correctly matched with a corresponding closing delimiter. This requires the parser to maintain context—often via recursive calls—and to generate meaningful error messages if the nesting is unbalanced.

For example, consider an expression with multiple nested parentheses:

```
(3 + (4 * (5 - 2)))
```

The parser must correctly associate the inner and outer parentheses, generating a nested AST that reflects the hierarchical nature of the operations. Semantic actions for nested expressions should not only compute or record the values but also retain the structure, so that subsequent phases (like optimization or code generation) can traverse the tree in the intended order.

Nested Blocks in Structured Programming

Beyond expressions, entire blocks of code are often nested in languages that support structured programming. Nested blocks allow for the definition of local scopes, control flow structures, and even the definition of inner functions or classes. Parsing these blocks requires the parser to distinguish between different levels of nesting and to manage the corresponding symbol tables.

A typical grammar rule for a nested block might look like this:

```
block: '{' stmt_list '}' { $$ = create_block_node($2); }
    ;
```

Here, `stmt_list` might itself contain rules for nested blocks. The semantic action, `create_block_node()`, is responsible for encapsulating the list of statements and managing any necessary scope information. In many compilers, entering a new block involves pushing a new symbol table or scope context, and exiting the block involves popping that context. This mechanism ensures that identifiers declared within a block are not visible outside of it, preserving the language's scoping rules.

Case Study: Nested Control Structures

Consider a more advanced example from a C-like language that supports nested control structures such as loops and conditionals. A fragment of the grammar might look like this:

```
stmt: compound_stmt
    | if_stmt
```

```
    | while_stmt
    | expression_stmt
    ;


if_stmt: IF '(' expr ')' stmt {
        $$ = create_if_node($3, $5, NULL);
    }
    | IF '(' expr ')' stmt ELSE stmt {
        $$ = create_if_node($3, $5, $7);
    }
    ;


while_stmt: WHILE '(' expr ')' stmt {
        $$ = create_while_node($3, $5);
    }
    ;
```

In this example, each statement (stmt) may itself be a compound statement containing nested control structures. The semantic actions—such as create_if_node() and create_while_node()—not only build nodes in the AST but also link the nested structures correctly. By designing the grammar and semantic actions in this way, the parser can handle arbitrarily deep nesting of control structures, making it suitable for real-world programming languages.

7.4 Parsing Function Calls and Parameters

The Complexity of Function Calls

Function calls are a ubiquitous element in most programming languages. They often involve a mix of nested expressions, parameter lists, and even higher-order constructs such as function pointers or lambda expressions. Parsing function calls presents unique challenges because the grammar must distinguish between the function identifier, the argument list, and any surrounding syntactic elements (such as parentheses or commas).

Defining the Grammar for Function Calls

A typical grammar rule for a function call might look like the following:

```
function_call: IDENTIFIER '(' argument_list ')' { $$ = create_func_call_node($1, $3); }
    ;
```

```
argument_list: argument_list ',' expr { $$ = append_argument($1, $3); }
        | expr { $$ = create_argument_list($1); }
        | /* empty */ { $$ = create_empty_argument_list(); }
        ;
```

In this rule:

- **IDENTIFIER** represents the function name.
- The argument list is defined recursively so that it can handle a variable number of arguments separated by commas.
- Semantic actions such as `create_func_call_node()`, `append_argument()`, and `create_argument_list()` build an abstract syntax tree that accurately represents the function call, including its parameters.

Handling Optional Parameters and Overloading

In many modern languages, function calls can have optional parameters, default values, or even variable argument lists (varargs). The grammar must be flexible enough to accommodate these features. For instance, if a function call may include optional arguments, the argument list production can be modified to allow an empty list or a list with default values:

```
argument_list: argument_list ',' expr { $$ = append_argument($1, $3); }
        | expr { $$ = create_argument_list($1); }
        | /* empty */ { $$ = create_empty_argument_list(); }
        ;
```

Here, the production for an empty argument list handles the case where no parameters are provided. In a language with function overloading, the parser might need to use semantic actions to inspect the types of the arguments and choose the correct function signature. Although the parser's grammar might not directly encode overloading rules, the semantic actions can delegate this responsibility to later phases of the compiler.

Constructing the AST for Function Calls

When a function call is parsed, the semantic action should construct an AST node that contains the function identifier and a list of child nodes representing the arguments. A typical AST node for a function call might be structured as follows:

```
typedef struct ast_node {
   NodeType type;
   char *value;          // Function name for function call nodes
   struct ast_node *args;  // Linked list or array of argument nodes
   // Additional fields for location, type information, etc.
} ASTNode;
```

The semantic action for a function call would then create a node of type NODE_FUNC_CALL, assign the function name, and link the argument nodes. For example:

```
function_call: IDENTIFIER '(' argument_list ')' {
    $$ = create_func_call_node($1, $3);
}
;
```

The helper function create_func_call_node() is responsible for creating a node that captures all the relevant information about the function call, including its arguments and any necessary type-checking information.

Parsing Nested Function Calls

In many languages, function calls can be nested, meaning that a function call may appear as an argument to another function call. This increases the complexity of the parser because the grammar must be capable of handling such nesting without ambiguity. Consider the following example:

```
result = outer_func(inner_func(3, 4), 5);
```

Here, the parser must first recognize inner_func(3, 4) as a function call and then pass its result as an argument to outer_func(). A well-designed grammar with recursive argument list rules naturally supports this pattern. The parser uses recursion to process the inner call before constructing the outer call's AST node.

Dealing with Function Pointers and Anonymous Functions

Advanced languages may also support function pointers, lambda expressions, or anonymous functions. Parsing these constructs requires the grammar to handle function call syntax differently from regular calls. For example, lambda expressions might be enclosed in special delimiters or use different keywords. The grammar could have separate productions for function calls and lambda expressions, or it might use a shared production with different semantic actions based on context. Consider the following example:

```
lambda_expr: '[' parameter_list ']' '{' stmt_list '}' {
    $$ = create_lambda_node($2, $4);
}
;
```

In this case, the lambda expression production creates a node that represents an anonymous function. This node might then be used as an argument in a function call or assigned to a variable. The flexibility of YACC's semantic actions allows you to integrate these advanced features seamlessly into your language's syntax.

Semantic Analysis During Function Call Parsing

During the parsing of function calls, it is often useful to perform early semantic analysis. For example, when a function call is encountered, the parser can verify that the function is declared, that the number of arguments matches the function's signature, and that the argument types are compatible. While comprehensive semantic analysis is typically handled in later phases of the compiler, integrating preliminary checks during parsing can lead to more informative error messages and prevent cascading errors.

Consider the following pseudo-code within a semantic action:

```
function_call: IDENTIFIER '(' argument_list ')' {
    Symbol *funcSym = lookup_function($1);
    if (funcSym == NULL) {
        yyerror("Undefined function");
        $$ = create_error_node("undefined_function");
    } else if (!validate_arguments(funcSym, $3)) {
        yyerror("Argument type mismatch");
        $$ = create_error_node("arg_type_error");
    } else {
        $$ = create_func_call_node($1, $3);
    }
}
;
```

In this example, the semantic action consults the symbol table and performs type checking on the argument list before constructing the AST node. This approach enhances the robustness of the parser and provides immediate feedback to the programmer.

7.5 Implementing Error Productions

The Role of Error Productions in Robust Parsing

No matter how well a grammar is designed, real-world input is bound to contain errors. A robust parser must not only detect syntax errors but also recover from them gracefully so that it can continue parsing and provide useful diagnostic messages. Error productions are a mechanism provided by YACC to incorporate error handling directly into the grammar, allowing the parser to skip over erroneous input and resume processing.

Defining the Error Token

YACC reserves a special token called error that can be inserted into grammar rules to trigger error recovery. By strategically placing the error token in your productions, you can tell the parser how to behave when it encounters unexpected input. For example, consider a rule for a statement:

```
statement: error ';' { yyerror("Skipping invalid statement"); }
    | valid_statement
    ;
```

Here, if the parser cannot match valid_statement, it will use the production with the error token. This rule instructs the parser to skip input until a semicolon is encountered, thereby resynchronizing with the input stream and allowing parsing to continue.

Strategies for Error Recovery

Error recovery strategies vary depending on the language and the severity of the error. Some common approaches include:

- **Panic Mode Recovery:** In this method, the parser discards input tokens until it finds a synchronizing token (such as a semicolon or closing brace). This is a simple and effective technique that prevents one error from causing a cascade of subsequent errors.
- **Phrase-Level Recovery:** Instead of discarding a large portion of the input, phrase-level recovery attempts to correct a small part of the input by inserting, deleting, or replacing tokens. This approach can be more user-friendly but is also more complex to implement.
- **Error Productions with Recovery:** By embedding the error token into the grammar, you can provide custom recovery rules that limit the extent of error propagation. These productions often include semantic actions that log the error, create special error nodes in the AST, or even attempt to fill in missing parts of the input.

Crafting Effective Error Productions

When designing error productions, it is important to balance between recovering from errors and preventing misinterpretation of the input. The goal is to allow the parser to continue processing while clearly indicating that an error occurred. Here is an example of an error production for a compound statement:

```
compound_stmt: '{' stmt_list '}' { $$ = create_compound_node($2); }
    | '{' error '}' { yyerror("Error in block; skipping contents"); $$ = create_error_node("block_error"); }
    ;
```

In this rule, if an error is encountered within a block, the parser logs the error and creates an error node. This node can later be used to generate an error message during code generation or semantic analysis.

Incorporating Error Nodes into the AST

One advanced technique in error recovery is to integrate error nodes directly into the abstract syntax tree (AST). Instead of discarding erroneous input completely, the parser builds an AST that includes nodes representing errors. This approach has several advantages:

- **Comprehensive Diagnostics:** The AST can be traversed later to produce detailed error reports, showing exactly where and how the input deviated from the expected syntax.
- **Partial Analysis:** Even if parts of the input are erroneous, the AST may still contain valid subtrees that can be analyzed or optimized. This is particularly useful in interactive development environments where immediate feedback is important.
- **Graceful Degradation:** By embedding error nodes, the compiler can continue to process and perhaps even generate code for the correct parts of the program. This is essential in systems where multiple errors are reported in a single compilation cycle.

A typical semantic action for an error production might look like this:

```
assignment: IDENTIFIER ASSIGN expr {
  if (!validate_assignment($1, $3)) {
    yyerror("Type mismatch in assignment");
    $$ = create_error_node("assignment_error");
  } else {
    $$ = create_assignment_node($1, $3);
  }
}
;
```

In this example, if the assignment is invalid, the semantic action logs an error and returns an error node. This node becomes part of the AST, allowing later phases of the compiler to be aware of the error.

Advanced Techniques in Error Recovery

Some modern parsing systems implement more sophisticated error recovery strategies that go beyond simple panic mode. These techniques include:

- **Token Insertion and Deletion:** The parser may try to "guess" missing tokens by inserting them into the token stream or by ignoring extraneous tokens. This requires careful tuning to avoid masking serious errors.
- **Error-Correcting Parsing:** In some systems, the parser uses probabilistic models or heuristic rules to determine the most likely corrections for an error. This approach can significantly improve the quality of error messages and the overall robustness of the parser, but it also increases complexity.
- **Context-Sensitive Recovery:** By using information from the surrounding context, the parser can sometimes determine whether an error is localized or indicative of a larger problem. For example, if an operator is missing between two expressions, the parser might insert a default operator (like a plus sign) and log a warning instead of a hard error.

Debugging Error Productions

Testing error recovery is as important as testing correct input. When designing error productions, it is critical to create a comprehensive set of test cases that include malformed input. Use debugging output (such as logging inside semantic actions) to trace how the parser recovers from errors. Tools like Valgrind and GDB can help identify memory issues and logic errors in the error recovery code.

Chapter 8: Building a Complete Compiler Frontend

A compiler frontend is responsible for reading the source code of a programming language, breaking it down into tokens, analyzing its grammatical structure, performing semantic checks, and ultimately generating an intermediate representation (IR) for further processing (such as optimization and code generation). In this chapter, we explain how to build a complete compiler frontend using FLEX and YACC. While previous chapters have introduced the basics of lexical analysis, parsing, and advanced translation techniques, here we synthesize these concepts into a comprehensive frontend design.

8.1 Overview of Compiler Frontend Architecture

High-Level Architecture

A complete compiler frontend is composed of several interrelated components that work in tandem to transform raw source code into a structured representation. At a high level, the frontend comprises:

- **Lexical Analyzer (Lexer):** Uses FLEX to scan the source code, matching patterns defined by regular expressions. The lexer transforms a stream of characters into a sequence of tokens (keywords, operators, identifiers, etc.).
- **Syntax Analyzer (Parser):** Uses YACC to process the token stream according to a formal grammar. The parser builds a parse tree (or abstract syntax tree) that represents the syntactic structure of the program.
- **Semantic Analyzer:** Embeds semantic actions within the grammar rules to perform type checking, enforce language constraints, and annotate the parse tree with semantic information.
- **Symbol Table Manager:** Manages the storage and retrieval of identifiers, tracks scope, and holds type and declaration information.

- **Intermediate Representation (IR) Generator:** Translates the annotated parse tree into a machine- or platform-independent intermediate code that can be passed to later stages (such as optimization and code generation).

Design Considerations

When designing the compiler frontend, several key factors must be taken into account:

- **Modularity:** Each component should be as independent as possible. A well-defined interface between the lexer and parser (via tokens and semantic values) allows for easier debugging and future modifications.
- **Error Handling:** The frontend must detect and recover from errors gracefully. Early error detection—both in the lexical and syntactic phases—helps prevent cascading failures.
- **Performance:** Both FLEX and YACC are designed for high efficiency. However, when integrated, the design must ensure that recursive parsing or deep semantic actions do not degrade performance.
- **Extensibility:** As languages evolve, the compiler frontend must be able to accommodate new language features. The design should permit changes to grammar rules, symbol management, and semantic actions with minimal re-engineering.
- **Maintainability:** Clear documentation, consistent naming conventions, and modular code organization are essential to maintain and extend the compiler frontend over time.

The End-to-End Flow

The overall flow of a compiler frontend is as follows:

1. **Input:** The source code is fed into the lexer.
2. **Lexical Analysis:** FLEX processes the input and emits tokens. Each token may include a semantic value (e.g., numeric literals, identifier names).
3. **Parsing:** YACC receives tokens from the lexer, applies grammar rules, and builds a parse tree. Semantic actions embedded in the grammar add meaning to the tree.
4. **Semantic Analysis:** Type checking, scope verification, and symbol resolution are performed. This phase may annotate the AST with error flags and type information.
5. **Intermediate Representation:** The semantic tree is then translated into an intermediate form (such as three-address code), which serves as the input to the backend.
6. **Output:** The final output of the frontend is the IR along with symbol table information and error reports.

This chapter will provide detailed guidance for each of these steps.

8.2 Lexical Analysis with FLEX: From Source Code to Tokens

Introduction to Lexical Analysis

Lexical analysis is the process of reading the raw source code and breaking it into a meaningful sequence of tokens. Tokens are the basic building blocks of the language—they can be keywords, identifiers, literals, operators, and punctuation. FLEX is a tool that automates this process by allowing you to specify regular expressions that match these tokens.

Setting Up the FLEX Environment

Before you begin writing the lexer, you need to set up a well-organized project structure. For example, your directory might include:

```
src/
  lexer.l
  common.h
  ...
```

The file **lexer.l** contains the FLEX specification, and **common.h** includes shared definitions such as token constants. A typical header might look like:

```
#ifndef COMMON_H
#define COMMON_H


enum yytokentype {
    NUMBER = 258,
    IDENTIFIER,
    KEYWORD_IF,
    KEYWORD_ELSE,
    PLUS,
    MINUS,
    MULTIPLY,
    DIVIDE,
    LPAREN,
    RPAREN,
    LBRACE,
    RBRACE,
    SEMICOLON,
    ASSIGN,
    // Add more tokens as needed.
};

#endif /* COMMON_H */
```

Writing the FLEX Specification

A FLEX file consists of three sections: definitions, rules, and user code. The definitions section includes C code and header inclusions. The rules section specifies regular expressions and associated actions. Finally, the user code section includes functions like yywrap().

Here's an example of a FLEX file for a simple language:

```
%{
#include "common.h"
#include <stdlib.h>
#include <stdio.h>
#include "symtable.h"  // Optional, for symbol table integration.
%}


/* Regular expression definitions */
DIGIT      [0-9]
LETTER     [a-zA-Z_]
ID         {LETTER}({LETTER}|{DIGIT})*


%%


{DIGIT}+  {
    /* Convert the lexeme to an integer value */
    yylval = atoi(yytext);
    return NUMBER;
}


{ID}      {
    /* Check if the lexeme is a reserved keyword */
    int token = lookup_reserved(yytext);
    if (token == IDENTIFIER) {
        /* Optionally, insert the identifier into the symbol table */
        Symbol *sym = lookup_symbol(yytext);
        if (sym == NULL)
            sym = insert_symbol(yytext, 0);  // 0 could denote an undefined type.
        yylval = (int)sym;
    }
    return token;
}


"if"    { return KEYWORD_IF; }
"else"    { return KEYWORD_ELSE; }
```

```
"+"      { return PLUS; }
"-"      { return MINUS; }
"*"      { return MULTIPLY; }
"/"      { return DIVIDE; }
"("      { return LPAREN; }
")"      { return RPAREN; }
"{"      { return LBRACE; }
"}"      { return RBRACE; }
";"      { return SEMICOLON; }
"="      { return ASSIGN; }


[ \t\n]+   { /* Skip whitespace */ }
.          { printf("Unexpected character: %s\n", yytext); }



%%


int yywrap(void) {
    return 1;
}
```

Key Considerations in Lexical Analysis

Pattern Matching and Regular Expressions

The strength of FLEX lies in its ability to match patterns using regular expressions. Each rule specifies a pattern and an action. For example, $[0-9]+$ matches one or more digits. The action converts the text to an integer and returns the token type. The use of macros (such as DIGIT, LETTER, and ID) improves maintainability and readability.

Token Prioritization and Ambiguity

When multiple rules match the same input, FLEX uses the rule that appears first in the file. Therefore, it is essential to order rules carefully—reserved keywords should be checked before the general identifier rule to avoid misclassification.

Passing Semantic Values

Each token can carry additional information using the global variable yylval. In our example, numeric literals are converted and stored, and identifiers are associated with entries in the symbol table. This mechanism is critical for ensuring that the parser has access to all necessary data.

Integrating with the Build Process

After writing your FLEX specification, integrate it into your build system (for example, via a Makefile). The build system should automatically invoke FLEX to generate a C source file (commonly named lex.yy.c), which is then compiled along with the rest of your code. A snippet from the Makefile might look like:

```
lex.yy.c: src/lexer.l src/common.h
        flex -o lex.yy.c src/lexer.l
```

Debugging the Lexer

While developing your lexer, embed debugging print statements in the actions. For instance, printing out the matched token and its value helps confirm that your patterns and conversions are working correctly. Later, these debug statements can be removed or disabled for production builds.

8.3 Syntax Analysis with YACC: Building the Parse Tree

Overview of YACC Parsing

YACC is a parser generator that reads a formal grammar and produces a C source file for a parser. Unlike the lexer, which processes the raw character stream, the parser works on the token stream provided by the lexer. The parser's job is to determine whether the sequence of tokens conforms to the language's syntax and to construct a corresponding parse tree or abstract syntax tree (AST).

Setting Up the YACC File

A typical YACC file is divided into three sections:

1. **Definitions Section:** Contains C code, includes, token declarations, and precedence rules.
2. **Rules Section:** Defines the grammar productions and embeds semantic actions.
3. **User Code Section:** Contains additional C functions (such as main() and error handling routines).

An example of a basic YACC file is:

```
%{
#include <stdio.h>
#include <stdlib.h>
#include "common.h"
#include "symtable.h"
#include "ast.h"    // Header for AST node definitions.
```

```
void yyerror(const char *s);
%}


%token NUMBER IDENTIFIER KEYWORD_IF KEYWORD_ELSE PLUS MINUS
MULTIPLY DIVIDE LPAREN RPAREN LBRACE RBRACE SEMICOLON ASSIGN


/* Define precedence and associativity to resolve conflicts */
%left '+' '-'
%left '*' '/'


%%


program:
    stmt_list { $$ = create_program_node($1); }
    ;


stmt_list:
    stmt_list stmt { $$ = append_statement($1, $2); }
  | stmt { $$ = create_statement_list($1); }
    ;


stmt:
    compound_stmt
  | if_stmt
  | expression_stmt
    ;


compound_stmt:
    LBRACE stmt_list RBRACE { $$ = create_compound_node($2); }
    ;


if_stmt:
    KEYWORD_IF LPAREN expression RPAREN stmt { $$ = create_if_node($3, $5,
NULL); }
  | KEYWORD_IF LPAREN expression RPAREN stmt KEYWORD_ELSE stmt
{ $$ = create_if_node($3, $5, $7); }
    ;


expression_stmt:
    expression SEMICOLON { $$ = create_expr_stmt($1); }
```

```
    ;


expression:
    expression PLUS expression { $$ = create_operator_node("+", $1, $3); }
    | expression MINUS expression { $$ = create_operator_node("-", $1, $3); }
    | expression MULTIPLY expression { $$ = create_operator_node("*", $1, $3); }
    | expression DIVIDE expression {
        if    ($3    ==    0)    {    yyerror("Division    by    zero");    $$    =
create_error_node("division_by_zero"); }
        else { $$ = create_operator_node("/", $1, $3); }
    }
    | LPAREN expression RPAREN { $$ = $2; }
    | NUMBER { $$ = create_leaf_node(NUMBER, $1); }
    | IDENTIFIER { $$ = create_leaf_node(IDENTIFIER, $1); }
    ;



%%


void yyerror(const char *s) {
    fprintf(stderr, "Syntax error: %s\n", s);
}


int main(void) {
    printf("Enter source code:\n");
    yyparse();
    return 0;
}
```

Grammar Design and Production Rules

The grammar defined above is designed to handle a simple programming language with compound statements, conditional statements, and arithmetic expressions. Notice the use of recursive rules in stmt_list and expression—this allows the parser to build a hierarchical tree that mirrors the nested structure of the source code.

Semantic Actions and AST Construction

Semantic actions are embedded in the grammar rules to perform the translation from a sequence of tokens into an abstract syntax tree. For example, when an arithmetic operation is encountered, the action create_operator_node("+", $1, $3) is called. This function (defined elsewhere in your code) creates a new AST node representing the addition operation and links the left and right subtrees.

The AST is the backbone of the compiler frontend, as it abstracts away syntactic details and provides a structured representation of the program for further semantic analysis.

Conflict Resolution and Precedence Declarations

YACC often encounters conflicts when multiple productions could apply to a given token sequence. The use of %left declarations for operators helps resolve these conflicts by specifying operator precedence and associativity. In our example, multiplication and division have higher precedence than addition and subtraction, ensuring that the parse tree reflects the correct order of operations.

Integration with the Lexer

The parser communicates with the lexer through the function yylex(). Each time YACC requires a new token, it calls yylex(), which was generated by FLEX. The tokens returned by the lexer (along with their semantic values stored in yylval) are then processed by the grammar rules.

Error Handling in the Parser

Error handling is critical in syntax analysis. The function yyerror() is called whenever the parser encounters an unexpected token or a violation of the grammar. Proper error messages guide the user in correcting the source code and help maintain the robustness of the compiler frontend.

Testing the Parser

A key aspect of building the parser is thorough testing. Test cases should include both valid and invalid input to ensure that the grammar and semantic actions behave as expected. Unit tests can be written for each production, and integrated testing should verify that the entire system constructs the correct AST for a given source file.

8.4 Semantic Actions and Type Checking: Enforcing Language Rules

Role of Semantic Analysis

Once the parser has built a syntactic representation of the source code, the next step is to perform semantic analysis. This phase checks the program for semantic consistency—ensuring that types match, variables are declared before use, and operations are performed on compatible types. Semantic actions embedded in the YACC grammar are used to enforce these rules and annotate the AST with type and scope information.

Embedding Semantic Actions

In our YACC rules, semantic actions are specified within curly braces. These actions not only build AST nodes but also perform type checking. For example, consider the rule for arithmetic expressions:

```
expression:
    expression PLUS expression {
        if (check_numeric($1) && check_numeric($3))
            $$ = create_operator_node("+", $1, $3);
        else {
            yyerror("Type error: Non-numeric operand for '+'");
            $$ = create_error_node("type_error");
        }
    }
```

Here, before constructing an operator node, the semantic action calls a helper function check_numeric() to verify that both operands are numeric. If the check fails, an error is reported and an error node is created.

Type Systems and AST Annotation

For languages with richer type systems, the semantic analysis phase must handle type inference, coercion, and compatibility checks. The AST nodes can be extended to include type information. For example:

```
typedef struct ast_node {
    NodeType type;
    char *value;
    struct ast_node *left;
    struct ast_node *right;
    int dataType; // e.g., INTEGER, FLOAT, etc.
} ASTNode;
```

During semantic actions, after constructing a node, you can assign a type to it based on the types of its children. Type-checking functions can then enforce that the types match for operations like arithmetic and logical comparisons.

Handling Declarations and Assignments

Declarations and assignments are critical points where semantic checks are enforced. For example, when processing a variable declaration, the semantic action should insert the identifier into the symbol table with its declared type. An assignment statement should then check that the variable has been declared and that the type of the assigned value is compatible with the variable's type.

A simplified rule for assignment might be:

```
assignment:
    IDENTIFIER ASSIGN expression {
        Symbol *sym = (Symbol *)$1;
        if (sym == NULL) {
            yyerror("Undeclared variable in assignment");
            $$ = create_error_node("undeclared");
        } else if (!compatible(sym->type, $3->dataType)) {
            yyerror("Type mismatch in assignment");
            $$ = create_error_node("type_mismatch");
        } else {
            $$ = create_assignment_node(sym, $3);
        }
    }
;
```

Flow of Semantic Analysis

Semantic analysis typically follows these steps:

1. **Annotation:** As the parser builds the AST, semantic actions annotate nodes with type and scope information. Each node may carry metadata such as the data type of an expression or the scope level of a variable.
2. **Validation:** Semantic checks verify that the program adheres to the language rules. This includes ensuring that operations are performed on compatible types, that functions are called with the correct number and type of arguments, and that control structures (like loops and conditionals) are semantically valid.
3. **Error Reporting:** When a semantic error is detected, the semantic action invokes yyerror () to log the issue. The creation of error nodes in the AST allows the compiler frontend to continue processing the remainder of the program, providing comprehensive error feedback to the user.

Advanced Type Checking Techniques

For languages that support polymorphism or user-defined types, semantic actions must be more sophisticated. Techniques such as type inference (deducing the type of an expression based on context) or overloading resolution (choosing the correct function or operator based on argument types) may be necessary. These techniques often require:

- **Type Environments:** A type environment is a mapping from identifiers to their types. This environment is maintained during semantic analysis and updated as new declarations are processed.
- **Type Unification:** In languages with generics or polymorphism, type unification algorithms are used to determine whether two type expressions can be made equivalent through substitution.
- **Error Recovery in Type Checking:** If a type mismatch occurs, the semantic action may attempt to recover by inserting coercion nodes or by generating a

special error type. This allows further analysis to continue without being derailed by a single error.

Practical Considerations

Semantic actions and type checking are often the most challenging parts of compiler frontend development. They require a deep understanding of the language's semantics and careful design to ensure that errors are caught early. Robust testing of semantic actions is essential—test cases should include both valid programs and programs designed to trigger specific type errors.

8.5 Symbol Table and Scope Management: Tracking Identifiers

Importance of the Symbol Table

A symbol table is a central repository that stores information about identifiers—such as variable names, function names, and their associated types and scopes. It is essential for ensuring that each identifier is declared before use, that declarations do not conflict, and that scope rules are enforced correctly.

Designing the Symbol Table

The symbol table is typically implemented as a hash table for fast lookup. A basic symbol entry might be defined as follows:

```
typedef struct Symbol {
    char *name;
    int type;        // Data type or other attributes.
    int scopeLevel;   // The depth of the scope.
    // Additional fields, e.g., memory location, function parameters, etc.
    struct Symbol *next;
} Symbol;
```

The symbol table itself may be implemented as an array of pointers (hash buckets), and scope management can be handled using a stack of symbol tables or by maintaining a scope level field.

Inserting and Looking Up Symbols

During the lexical and parsing phases, when an identifier is encountered, the compiler must check if it exists in the symbol table. If it is a declaration, it is inserted; if it is a usage, it is looked up for type checking and further processing. For example, in the lexer:

```
[a-zA-Z_][a-zA-Z0-9_]* {
    int token = lookup_reserved(yytext);
```

```
    if (token == IDENTIFIER) {
        Symbol *sym = lookup_symbol(yytext);
        if (sym == NULL)
            sym = insert_symbol(yytext, /* default type */ 0);
        yylval = (int)sym;
    }
    return token;
}
```

In the parser, as seen in assignment rules, the symbol is retrieved from yylval and used for semantic analysis.

Scope Management

Scope management is critical for languages with block structures. Each time the parser enters a new block (for example, a compound statement), a new scope should be created. When exiting the block, the scope should be destroyed so that local identifiers do not leak into the outer scope.

One common method is to implement scope management with a stack:

- **Entering a Scope:** Push a new symbol table (or increase a scope level counter) onto the stack.
- **Exiting a Scope:** Pop the symbol table from the stack, deallocating any symbols that were only valid in that scope.

For example, in the parser's semantic action for a compound statement:

```
compound_stmt:
    LBRACE { enter_scope(); }
    stmt_list
    RBRACE { exit_scope(); $$ = create_compound_node($2); }
    ;
```

The functions enter_scope() and exit_scope() manage the symbol table stack. This ensures that each variable is only visible within the block in which it is declared.

Advanced Symbol Table Features

For more complex languages, the symbol table may need to support additional features:

- **Function Overloading:** The table should be able to store multiple entries for functions with the same name but different parameter types.
- **Namespaces and Classes:** For object-oriented languages, symbol tables must handle class scopes, inheritance, and member resolution.
- **Type Aliases and Templates:** Support for user-defined types, generics, and type aliases requires a more flexible symbol table design.

Implementing these features typically involves extending the basic symbol entry structure and maintaining additional metadata in the symbol table.

Integration with Semantic Actions

In the semantic actions, the symbol table is used to validate declarations and resolve references. For example, during a variable declaration, the parser might perform the following steps:

1. Check if the identifier already exists in the current scope.
2. If it does, generate an error indicating a duplicate declaration.
3. Otherwise, insert the new symbol into the table with its declared type.

Similarly, when an identifier is used, the semantic action looks it up in the symbol table and retrieves its type for type checking.

Practical Example: Symbol Table in a Mini Language

Consider a scenario in which a mini programming language supports variable declarations and assignments. A typical declaration rule might be:

```
declaration:
    IDENTIFIER {
        Symbol *sym = (Symbol *)$1;
        if (is_declared_in_current_scope(sym->name)) {
            yyerror("Duplicate declaration");
            $$ = create_error_node("duplicate_declaration");
        } else {
            set_symbol_type(sym, current_type);
            $$ = create_declaration_node(sym);
        }
    }
    ;
```

Here, the function `is_declared_in_current_scope()` checks if the identifier is already declared. The function `set_symbol_type()` assigns the declared type to the symbol. This integration ensures that the symbol table reflects the program's structure and that semantic errors are caught early.

8.6 Generating Intermediate Representations: Bridging to the Backend

Role of Intermediate Representations (IR)

After the frontend has parsed and semantically analyzed the source code, the next step is to generate an intermediate representation (IR). The IR is a lower-level, machine-independent code that serves as the input to the optimization and code generation phases of the compiler. By decoupling the frontend from the backend, the IR enables multiple target architectures to be supported with a common analysis framework.

Types of Intermediate Representations

There are various types of IRs, including:

- **Abstract Syntax Trees (ASTs):** These are high-level, hierarchical representations of the source program. ASTs capture the structure and semantics of the code but may be too abstract for direct code generation.
- **Three-Address Code (TAC):** TAC represents the program as a sequence of simple instructions, each typically containing at most three operands. It is well-suited for optimization and can be translated to various target architectures.
- **Control Flow Graphs (CFGs):** CFGs represent the flow of control within a program and are useful for data-flow analysis and optimizations such as dead code elimination.

Building the IR in the Compiler Frontend

The process of generating the IR involves traversing the AST and converting it into a more linear, low-level representation. This is often done as a separate phase after semantic analysis, but it can also be integrated into semantic actions. For example, instead of simply creating an AST node for an arithmetic expression, a semantic action might generate the corresponding three-address code.

Consider a semantic action for an arithmetic expression:

```
expression:
    expression PLUS expression {
        $$ = generate_tac("+", $1, $3);
    }
  | NUMBER { $$ = generate_tac_from_number($1); }
  ;
```

The function `generate_tac()` would create a new temporary variable, generate the code to perform the addition, and return a representation that encapsulates the operation. This representation is then propagated up the parse tree until the entire program is translated into IR.

Techniques for IR Generation

There are several techniques used in IR generation:

- **Tree Traversal:** A common approach is to perform a post-order traversal of the AST, generating IR code for each node as it is visited. This ensures that the operands of an operation are processed before the operation itself.

- **Direct Generation in Semantic Actions:** In this method, the IR code is generated inline as the parser reduces productions. This can simplify the pipeline but may complicate the semantic actions.
- **Intermediate Data Structures:** Some compiler frontends build intermediate data structures (such as symbol tables and flow graphs) that assist in generating the IR. These structures can capture additional information, such as variable lifetimes and control flow details.

Managing Temporary Variables

One of the challenges in IR generation is the management of temporary variables. When translating complex expressions, intermediate results are stored in temporary variables. A temporary variable manager is often implemented to generate unique variable names and to recycle variables where possible. For example, a helper function might generate names like t1, t2, etc., ensuring that each temporary is unique within the IR.

Example: Generating Three-Address Code

Consider an example of generating TAC for a simple arithmetic expression such as a + b * c. The IR generation might proceed as follows:

Process b * c: Generate code:

```
t1 = b * c
```

Process a + t1: Generate code:

```
t2 = a + t1
```

The final IR is a sequence of TAC instructions:

```
t1 = b * c
t2 = a + t1
```

Semantic actions can be written to generate these instructions as the parser reduces the expression productions. This IR can then be passed to the optimization phase or directly translated into target code.

IR Optimization Considerations

Once the IR is generated, it is common to apply optimizations such as constant folding, common subexpression elimination, and dead code elimination. Although these optimizations are typically part of the backend, the design of the IR should facilitate such transformations. Keeping the IR in a simple, three-address code format can make these optimizations easier to implement.

Integrating IR Generation into the Frontend

The integration of IR generation into the compiler frontend involves a few key steps:

- **AST Traversal:** Once the AST is fully constructed and semantically analyzed, traverse it to generate IR instructions.
- **Semantic Actions for IR:** Alternatively, embed IR generation into the semantic actions so that each production directly emits IR code.
- **IR Data Structures:** Design data structures to store the IR, such as arrays or linked lists of instruction objects. Each instruction object might contain fields for the operator, operands, and result.
- **Debugging the IR:** Provide facilities to print or visualize the generated IR. This is critical for verifying that the frontend is producing the correct intermediate code.

Practical Example: A Mini Compiler Frontend

To illustrate IR generation, consider a mini compiler that handles arithmetic expressions and assignments. The semantic action for an assignment might be:

```
assignment:
    IDENTIFIER ASSIGN expression SEMICOLON {
        Symbol *sym = (Symbol *)$1;
        IRInstruction *inst = generate_assignment(sym->name, $3);
        add_ir_instruction(inst);
        $$ = create_assignment_node(sym, $3);
    }
;
```

In this example, `generate_assignment()` creates an IR instruction that assigns the result of the expression (represented by $3) to the variable, and `add_ir_instruction()` appends the instruction to a global list. The resulting IR is a sequence of instructions that mirror the structure of the input program.

8.7 Integration, Testing, and Debugging: Ensuring a Robust Frontend

Integration Challenges

Once all components of the compiler frontend are implemented—lexer, parser, semantic analyzer, symbol table manager, and IR generator—they must be integrated into a single, cohesive system. Integration challenges include ensuring that data flows correctly between components, that error handling is consistent, and that the overall performance meets requirements.

End-to-End Testing

Testing the complete frontend involves creating a suite of test cases that cover all language constructs, including edge cases and error scenarios. Tests should include:

- **Lexical Tests:** Verify that the lexer correctly identifies tokens from various inputs.
- **Parsing Tests:** Ensure that the parser builds the correct parse tree or AST for valid input, and that it gracefully handles invalid input.
- **Semantic Tests:** Validate that type checking and other semantic analyses produce correct results and error messages.
- **IR Tests:** Confirm that the generated IR corresponds to the intended operations and that optimizations do not alter the semantics.

Debugging Techniques

Debugging a complete compiler frontend can be challenging due to the complexity of interactions between components. Some useful techniques include:

- **Verbose Mode:** Enable debugging output in both FLEX and YACC (e.g., by setting yydebug = 1) to trace token flow and parser actions.
- **Logging:** Insert logging statements in semantic actions, symbol table functions, and IR generation routines to record the state of the system.
- **Modular Testing:** Test each component independently before integrating them. For example, test the lexer with sample inputs, then test the parser with a fixed token stream.
- **Visualization Tools:** Use visualization tools to display the AST or IR. Graphical representations can reveal structural errors that are difficult to spot in raw text.

Performance Profiling

Performance is a key concern for compiler frontends, especially when processing large codebases. Use profiling tools (such as gprof or perf) to identify bottlenecks in lexical scanning, parsing, or IR generation. Optimize critical sections by refining regular expressions, simplifying grammar rules, or caching symbol table lookups.

Continuous Integration and Regression Testing

As the compiler frontend evolves, it is important to incorporate continuous integration (CI) practices. Automated build and test systems ensure that changes do not break existing functionality. A comprehensive regression test suite should be maintained, covering both expected behavior and error recovery. This approach provides confidence that the frontend remains robust as new language features are added.

8.8 Challenges, Best Practices, and Future Extensions

Common Challenges

Building a complete compiler frontend with FLEX and YACC presents several challenges:

- **Ambiguity and Conflict Resolution:** Designing an unambiguous grammar that correctly reflects the language semantics can be difficult. It may require extensive testing and fine-tuning of precedence rules.
- **Error Handling:** Implementing effective error detection and recovery mechanisms is crucial for user-friendly compilers. Balancing between strict error reporting and graceful recovery is a recurring challenge.
- **Integration of Semantic Analysis:** Semantic actions and type checking require a deep understanding of the language's rules. Bugs in these areas can lead to subtle errors that are hard to diagnose.
- **Maintaining Extensibility:** As the language evolves, the compiler frontend must be easily extensible. This requires a modular design and clear interfaces between components.

Best Practices

To overcome these challenges, consider the following best practices:

- **Modular Design:** Clearly separate the responsibilities of the lexer, parser, semantic analyzer, symbol table, and IR generator. Use well-defined interfaces to reduce interdependencies.
- **Consistent Naming Conventions:** Maintain consistency in naming tokens, non-terminals, functions, and variables. This enhances readability and maintainability.
- **Comprehensive Testing:** Develop a suite of test cases covering all aspects of the language. Use automated testing frameworks to run regression tests continuously.
- **Incremental Development:** Build the compiler frontend in stages, testing each component thoroughly before integration. Start with a minimal language subset and gradually add features.
- **Robust Error Reporting:** Provide informative error messages that help users understand and correct mistakes. Consider integrating context information, such as line numbers and source code snippets.
- **Documentation:** Document the design decisions, interfaces, and data structures used in the compiler frontend. Good documentation is invaluable for future maintenance and extension.

Future Extensions

Once a basic compiler frontend is complete, there are many directions for future enhancement:

- **Advanced Optimizations:** Implement optimizations on the IR, such as constant folding, loop unrolling, and dead code elimination.
- **Backend Integration:** Extend the frontend to interface with a code generation backend that produces target machine code or assembly.
- **Support for Additional Language Features:** Add support for complex language constructs such as classes, templates, exception handling, or concurrency.
- **Improved Error Recovery:** Explore advanced error recovery strategies that provide suggestions or auto-correct common mistakes.
- **User Interface Improvements:** Integrate the compiler frontend into an IDE or interactive environment to provide real-time feedback and error diagnostics.
- **Portability and Performance Enhancements:** Optimize the frontend for different platforms and improve memory usage and processing speed through profiling and refactoring.

Final Thoughts

Building a complete compiler frontend is a challenging but rewarding endeavor. By integrating FLEX for lexical analysis and YACC for parsing, and by incorporating robust semantic analysis and symbol management, you create a tool that forms the backbone of many modern language processing systems. The journey from raw source code to an intermediate representation is fraught with challenges—ambiguous grammars, error recovery, deep nesting, and type checking—but by following the practices outlined in this chapter, you can build a frontend that is efficient, maintainable, and extensible.

As you continue to develop your compiler frontend, remember that each component is a building block in a larger system. Refining the lexer and parser improves error detection; enhancing semantic actions strengthens type safety; and optimizing the IR generation paves the way for advanced backend processing. Each stage is interconnected, and improvements in one area often lead to benefits throughout the entire compilation process.

Moreover, the techniques discussed in this chapter are not limited to academic exercises. They form the core of many real-world compilers and interpreters, from small scripting languages to large-scale systems used in industry. By mastering these techniques, you position yourself to tackle the complexities of modern language design and implementation.

The journey of compiler construction is one of continual learning and adaptation. Technologies evolve, languages become more expressive, and the demands for efficient, reliable software increase. With a solid understanding of how to build a complete compiler frontend using FLEX and YACC, you are well-equipped to contribute to this dynamic field—whether by enhancing an existing language, creating a new one, or building tools that empower others to write better code.

Chapter 9: Case Studies and Practical Applications

In the world of compiler construction and language processing, theory meets practice in a multitude of projects. This chapter details several case studies that illustrate how the principles and techniques introduced in earlier chapters can be applied to solve real problems. Each project is chosen to demonstrate different facets of language processing, including arithmetic evaluation, language design, data interchange formats, and query processing. By studying these practical applications, you will gain insights into the challenges encountered during development and the strategies used to overcome them.

9.1 Implementing a Simple Calculator

A simple calculator is often the first project undertaken when exploring language processing. It serves as an excellent starting point because it encompasses all the essential components of a compiler frontend without excessive complexity. In this case study, we build a calculator that can handle basic arithmetic expressions, enforce operator precedence, and provide meaningful error messages.

Project Goals and Requirements

The main goals for the calculator project include:

- Reading an arithmetic expression from the user.
- Tokenizing the input using FLEX.
- Parsing the expression with YACC, ensuring correct handling of operator precedence and associativity.
- Evaluating the expression and displaying the result.
- Providing error detection (such as division by zero or syntax errors) and recovery.

Designing the Lexer

The lexer, implemented with FLEX, must recognize numeric literals, operators (such as $+, -, *, /$), and grouping symbols (parentheses). The design focuses on precise regular expressions and clear token definitions.

Token Definitions and Regular Expressions

We define tokens for numbers and operators in a common header file (e.g., common.h):

```
#ifndef COMMON_H
#define COMMON_H


enum yytokentype {
   NUMBER = 258,
   PLUS,
   MINUS,
   MULTIPLY,
   DIVIDE,
   LPAREN,
   RPAREN,
};


#endif /* COMMON_H */
```

In the FLEX file (calculator.l), we include the header and define patterns:

```
%{
#include "common.h"
#include <stdlib.h>
#include <stdio.h>
%}


/* Definitions for digit and number */
DIGIT   [0-9]
NUMBER  {DIGIT}+(\.{DIGIT}+)? /* Supports integers and decimals */


%%


{NUMBER} { yylval = atof(yytext); return NUMBER; }
"+"      { return PLUS; }
"-"      { return MINUS; }
"*"      { return MULTIPLY; }
```

```
"/"     { return DIVIDE; }
"("     { return LPAREN; }
")"     { return RPAREN; }
[ \t\n]+  { /* ignore whitespace */ }
.         { printf("Unexpected character: %s\n", yytext); }


%%


int yywrap(void) { return 1; }
```

Here, the lexer not only converts numeric text to a floating-point value but also prints out unexpected characters, helping the user detect mistakes.

Building the Parser

The parser, written with YACC (in calculator.y), uses the tokens from FLEX to build an abstract syntax tree (AST) and evaluate expressions. A key aspect is enforcing operator precedence through YACC's %left directives.

Grammar and Semantic Actions

The grammar is structured to handle arithmetic expressions:

```
%{
#include <stdio.h>
#include <stdlib.h>
#include "common.h"
void yyerror(const char *s);
%}


%token NUMBER PLUS MINUS MULTIPLY DIVIDE LPAREN RPAREN
%left '+' '-'
%left '*' '/'


%%


expression:
    expression PLUS expression { $$ = $1 + $3; }
  | expression MINUS expression { $$ = $1 - $3; }
  | expression MULTIPLY expression { $$ = $1 * $3; }
  | expression DIVIDE expression {
        if ($3 == 0) {
            yyerror("Division by zero");
```

```
            $$ = 0;
        } else {
            $$ = $1 / $3;
        }
    }
    | LPAREN expression RPAREN { $$ = $2; }
    | NUMBER { $$ = $1; }
    ;



%%



void yyerror(const char *s) {
    fprintf(stderr, "Error: %s\n", s);
}


int main(void) {
    printf("Enter an arithmetic expression:\n");
    yyparse();
    printf("Result: %lf\n", yylval);
    return 0;
}
```

This parser effectively builds a tree of arithmetic operations. The semantic actions perform the calculations during reduction. Note that error handling for division by zero is integrated directly into the production for division.

Testing and Debugging

Testing the calculator involves running it with various expressions, including:

- Valid expressions:
  - 3 + 4 * 2
  - (1 + 2) * (3 + 4)
  - 10 / 2 - 3
- Erroneous expressions:
  - 3 + * 4
  - 10 / 0

Verbose debugging output (enabled by setting yydebug = 1 in YACC) can help trace the parser's decisions.

Lessons Learned

Implementing the simple calculator project reveals several important points:

- **Modular Design:** Separating the lexer and parser simplifies troubleshooting.
- **Error Handling:** Immediate feedback for errors such as division by zero improves user experience.
- **Operator Precedence:** Correct precedence declarations are vital for evaluating expressions accurately.
- **Incremental Development:** Starting with a basic calculator and then extending it allows gradual complexity buildup.

9.2 Developing a Mini Programming Language

Overview

Building a mini programming language is a more ambitious project that takes the basic principles of lexical and syntax analysis to the next level. In this case study, we develop a small language that supports variable declarations, arithmetic operations, conditionals, and loops. The project highlights many advanced techniques such as symbol table management, scope handling, semantic analysis, and the construction of an abstract syntax tree (AST).

Language Design and Features

The mini language, which we will call "MiniLang," includes:

- **Variables and Assignments:** Support for declaring and using variables.
- **Arithmetic Expressions:** Complex expressions with proper operator precedence.
- **Control Structures:** if-else statements and while loops.
- **Block Structure:** Compound statements defined by curly braces to denote new scopes.

Lexical Analysis for MiniLang

The FLEX specification for MiniLang must recognize a wider range of tokens, including keywords (such as if, else, and while), identifiers, numeric literals, and punctuation.

Token Definitions

In the shared header (common.h), we define tokens:

```
#ifndef COMMON_H
#define COMMON_H


enum yytokentype {
  NUMBER = 258,
```

```
    IDENTIFIER,
    KEYWORD_IF,
    KEYWORD_ELSE,
    KEYWORD_WHILE,
    PLUS,
    MINUS,
    MULTIPLY,
    DIVIDE,
    ASSIGN,
    LPAREN,
    RPAREN,
    LBRACE,
    RBRACE,
    SEMICOLON,
};


#endif /* COMMON_H */
```

The FLEX File

A corresponding FLEX file (minilang. l) might include:

```
%{
#include "common.h"
#include <stdlib.h>
#include <stdio.h>
#include "symtable.h"
%}


DIGIT   [0-9]
LETTER  [a-zA-Z_]
ID      {LETTER}({LETTER}|{DIGIT})*


%%


"if"        { return KEYWORD_IF; }
"else"      { return KEYWORD_ELSE; }
"while"     { return KEYWORD_WHILE; }
{ID}        {
            // Check if identifier is a reserved keyword; if not, process as
IDENTIFIER.
            return IDENTIFIER;
        }
{DIGIT}+    { yylval = atoi(yytext); return NUMBER; }
```

```
"+"            { return PLUS; }
"-"            { return MINUS; }
"*"            { return MULTIPLY; }
"/"            { return DIVIDE; }
"="            { return ASSIGN; }
"("            { return LPAREN; }
")"            { return RPAREN; }
"{"            { return LBRACE; }
"}"            { return RBRACE;.}
";"            { return SEMICOLON; }
[ \t\n]+       { /* skip whitespace */ }
.              { printf("Unexpected character: %s\n", yytext); }
%%


int yywrap(void) { return 1; }
```

This lexer handles identifiers, numbers, and language keywords, setting the stage for more complex parsing in the next phase.

Syntax Analysis and AST Construction

The parser for MiniLang, defined in minilang.y, must handle a variety of statements and expressions.

Grammar Overview

A simplified grammar for MiniLang might be:

```
%{
#include <stdio.h>
#include <stdlib.h>
#include "common.h"
#include "ast.h"       // Contains definitions for AST nodes.
#include "symtable.h"  // Contains symbol table management functions.
void yyerror(const char *s);
%}


%token    NUMBER    IDENTIFIER    KEYWORD_IF    KEYWORD_ELSE
KEYWORD_WHILE PLUS MINUS MULTIPLY DIVIDE ASSIGN LPAREN RPAREN
LBRACE RBRACE SEMICOLON
%left '+' '-'
%left '*' '/'


%%
```

```
program:
    stmt_list { $$ = create_program_node($1); }
    ;


stmt_list:
    stmt_list stmt { $$ = append_statement($1, $2); }
  | stmt { $$ = create_statement_list($1); }
    ;



stmt:
    declaration
  | assignment_stmt
  | if_stmt
  | while_stmt
  | compound_stmt
  | expression_stmt
    ;


declaration:
    IDENTIFIER SEMICOLON {
       $$ = create_declaration_node($1);
       insert_symbol($1, /* default type */ 0);
    }
    ;


assignment_stmt:
    IDENTIFIER ASSIGN expression SEMICOLON {
       $$ = create_assignment_node($1, $3);
       update_symbol($1, $3->dataType);
    }
    ;


if_stmt:
    KEYWORD_IF LPAREN expression RPAREN stmt { $$ = create_if_node($3, $5,
NULL); }
  | KEYWORD_IF LPAREN expression RPAREN stmt KEYWORD_ELSE stmt
{ $$ = create_if_node($3, $5, $7); }
    ;


while_stmt:
```

```
    KEYWORD_WHILE   LPAREN   expression   RPAREN   stmt   {   $$   =
create_while_node($3, $5); }
    ;


compound_stmt:
    LBRACE stmt_list RBRACE { $$ = create_compound_node($2); }
    ;


expression_stmt:
    expression SEMICOLON { $$ = create_expr_stmt($1); }
    ;


expression:
    expression PLUS expression { $$ = create_operator_node("+", $1, $3); }
    | expression MINUS expression { $$ = create_operator_node("-", $1, $3); }
    | expression MULTIPLY expression { $$ = create_operator_node("*", $1, $3); }
    | expression DIVIDE expression {
        if ($3 == 0) {
            yyerror("Division by zero");
            $$ = create_error_node("division_by_zero");
        } else {
            $$ = create_operator_node("/", $1, $3);
        }
    }
    | LPAREN expression RPAREN { $$ = $2; }
    | NUMBER { $$ = create_leaf_node(NUMBER, $1); }
    | IDENTIFIER { $$ = create_leaf_node(IDENTIFIER, $1); }
    ;


%%


void yyerror(const char *s) {
    fprintf(stderr, "Syntax error: %s\n", s);
}


int main(void) {
    printf("Enter MiniLang source code:\n");
    yyparse();
    return 0;
}
```

AST and Semantic Actions

In MiniLang, every production rule is coupled with a semantic action that builds an AST. For instance, the production for an assignment statement calls `create_assignment_node()` to build a node that links the identifier with the computed expression. Declarations trigger symbol table insertions. By embedding these actions, the parser not only checks the syntactic correctness but also begins semantic analysis.

Scope and Symbol Table Management

MiniLang introduces scoping rules through compound statements. The parser should call functions like `enter_scope()` and `exit_scope()` when entering and leaving blocks. Although not shown explicitly here, these functions manage the symbol table so that variable declarations are correctly limited to their scope.

Testing and Debugging MiniLang

Testing MiniLang involves running source files that exercise all language features:

- **Valid Programs:** Programs with correct declarations, assignments, and control structures.
- **Error Cases:** Programs with undeclared variables, type mismatches, or syntax errors.

Using debugging output (from YACC's `yydebug` mode and additional logging in semantic actions) allows you to trace the AST construction and symbol table updates.

Lessons Learned

The development of MiniLang demonstrates:

- **Language Design:** Even a small language requires careful grammar design to support variables, control structures, and proper scoping.
- **Semantic Analysis Integration:** Embedding semantic actions in the parser helps catch errors early.
- **Symbol Table Management:** Maintaining a consistent symbol table across nested scopes is critical for a reliable language.
- **Extensibility:** Starting with a small language provides a foundation for adding more features over time.

9.3 Parsing JSON with FLEX and YACC

Introduction to JSON Parsing

JSON (JavaScript Object Notation) is a lightweight data interchange format that is widely used for configuration files, web APIs, and data storage. Although there are many dedicated JSON parsers available, building one using FLEX and YACC offers a great opportunity to apply parsing techniques to a real-world format. In this case study, we create a JSON parser that can handle objects, arrays, strings, numbers, booleans, and null.

JSON Grammar Overview

JSON's grammar is relatively simple but requires careful handling of nested objects and arrays. The basic elements include:

- **Objects:** Enclosed in braces { } with key/value pairs.
- **Arrays:** Enclosed in brackets [ ] with comma-separated values.
- **Values:** Can be strings, numbers, booleans (true, false), null, objects, or arrays.

Designing the Lexer for JSON

The FLEX specification for JSON must identify strings, numbers, punctuation (such as {, }, [,], :, and ,), and literals (true, false, null). In our JSON lexer (json. l), we define tokens accordingly.

Example FLEX Specification

```
%{
#include "common.h"
#include <stdlib.h>
#include <stdio.h>
%}


STRING     \"([^\\\"]|\\.)*\"
NUMBER     -?([0-9]+)(\.[0-9]+)?([eE][+-]?[0-9]+)?
%%


"{"        { return LBRACE; }
"}"        { return RBRACE; }
"["        { return LBRACKET; }
"]"        { return RBRACKET; }
":"        { return COLON; }
","        { return COMMA; }
true       { return TRUE; }
false      { return FALSE; }
null       { return NULLVAL; }
{NUMBER}   { yylval = atof(yytext); return NUMBER; }
{STRING}   {
             yylval = strdup(yytext);
             return STRING;
           }
[ \t\n]+   { /* Skip whitespace */ }
.          { printf("Unexpected character in JSON: %s\n", yytext); }
```

```
%%

int yywrap(void) { return 1; }
```

Here, tokens such as LBRACKET, RBRACKET, COLON, and COMMA are defined in common.h, along with TRUE, FALSE, and NULLVAL.

Building the JSON Parser

The YACC file for JSON (json.y) constructs a parse tree that mirrors the JSON structure. The grammar rules handle objects, arrays, and values.

Example YACC Specification for JSON

```
%{
#include <stdio.h>
#include <stdlib.h>
#include "common.h"
#include "json_ast.h" // Contains definitions for JSON AST nodes.
void yyerror(const char *s);
%}


%token STRING NUMBER LBRACE RBRACE LBRACKET RBRACKET COLON
COMMA TRUE FALSE NULLVAL


%%


json:
    value { $$ = $1; }
  ;


value:
    STRING { $$ = create_json_string($1); }
  | NUMBER { $$ = create_json_number($1); }
  | object { $$ = $1; }
  | array  { $$ = $1; }
  | TRUE   { $$ = create_json_bool(1); }
  | FALSE  { $$ = create_json_bool(0); }
  | NULLVAL { $$ = create_json_null(); }
  ;


object:
```

154

```
     LBRACE members RBRACE { $$ = create_json_object($2); }
   | LBRACE RBRACE { $$ = create_json_object_empty(); }
   ;


members:
    members COMMA pair { $$ = append_member($1, $3); }
  | pair { $$ = create_member_list($1); }
  ;


pair:
    STRING COLON value { $$ = create_json_pair($1, $3); }
  ;


array:
    LBRACKET elements RBRACKET { $$ = create_json_array($2); }
  | LBRACKET RBRACKET { $$ = create_json_array_empty(); }
  ;


elements:
    elements COMMA value { $$ = append_element($1, $3); }
  | value { $$ = create_element_list($1); }
  ;


%%


void yyerror(const char *s) {
   fprintf(stderr, "JSON Syntax error: %s\n", s);
}


int main(void) {
   printf("Enter JSON input:\n");
   yyparse();
   // Optionally, print or process the JSON AST here.
   return 0;
}
```

AST Construction and Semantic Actions

Each production calls helper functions such as create_json_object() or append_member() to construct a JSON AST. The AST represents the JSON structure and can be traversed later for evaluation, transformation, or serialization.

Testing the JSON Parser

Test your JSON parser with a variety of inputs:

- **Simple Objects:** { "name": "John", "age": 30 }
- **Nested Structures:** { "person": { "name": "Alice", "hobbies": ["reading", "coding"] } }
- **Arrays and Mixed Types:** [true, false, null, 123, "text", { "key": "value" }]

Thorough testing ensures that the parser correctly handles nesting and various JSON value types.

Challenges and Solutions

Parsing JSON with FLEX and YACC presents unique challenges:

- **String Escaping:** Properly handling escaped characters within strings requires careful regular expressions and additional processing in semantic actions.
- **Nested Structures:** Deeply nested objects or arrays require the parser to manage recursion without running into performance issues.
- **Error Recovery:** When encountering malformed JSON, the parser must provide meaningful error messages to guide corrections.

By addressing these challenges, the JSON parser case study demonstrates the versatility of FLEX and YACC in handling data interchange formats.

9.4 Handling XML and Markup Languages

Introduction to XML Parsing

XML (eXtensible Markup Language) is another widely used data format. Unlike JSON, XML has a more complex structure with start and end tags, attributes, and mixed content. Although dedicated XML parsers exist, implementing one using FLEX and YACC provides valuable insights into handling nested tags and recursive structures.

Grammar Design for XML

XML's grammar is inherently recursive. Elements can contain other elements, text, and attributes. A simplified grammar for XML might look like:

```
xml:
    element { $$ = $1; }
    ;

element:
```

```
    LANGLE NAME attributes RANGLE content LANGLE SLASH NAME RANGLE {
$$ = create_xml_element($2, $3, $5); }
    ;


attributes:
    attributes attribute { $$ = append_attribute($1, $2); }
    | /* empty */ { $$ = create_empty_attribute_list(); }
    ;


attribute:
    NAME EQUALS STRING { $$ = create_xml_attribute($1, $3); }
    ;


content:
    content element { $$ = append_content($1, $2); }
    | content TEXT { $$ = append_text($1, $2); }
    | /* empty */ { $$ = create_empty_content(); }
    ;
```

This grammar captures the essence of XML: nested elements, attributes, and mixed content. Note that the actual implementation in FLEX and YACC may require handling many edge cases.

The Lexer for XML

The XML lexer (xml.l) must recognize tags, attributes, and text. Special attention is needed for handling white space and character data.

Example XML Lexer

```
%{
#include "common.h"
#include <stdio.h>
#include <stdlib.h>
%}


NAME        [a-zA-Z_:][a-zA-Z0-9_.:-]*
STRING      \"([^\\\"]|\\.)*\"
TEXT        [^<]+


%%


"<"         { return LANGLE; }
```

```
"</"      { return LANGLE_SLASH; }
">"       { return RANGLE; }
"="       { return EQUALS; }
{NAME}    { yylval = strdup(yytext); return NAME; }
{STRING}  { yylval = strdup(yytext); return STRING; }
{TEXT}    { yylval = strdup(yytext); return TEXT; }
[ \t\n]+  { /* Ignore whitespace between tags */ }
.         { printf("Unexpected XML character: %s\n", yytext); }
%%


int yywrap(void) { return 1; }
```

Parsing XML with YACC

The YACC file for XML (xml.y) uses the tokens from the lexer to construct an XML DOM-like tree. Semantic actions are responsible for creating nodes for elements, attributes, and text.

Example YACC for XML

```
%{
#include <stdio.h>
#include <stdlib.h>
#include "common.h"
#include "xml_ast.h" // Contains definitions for XML nodes.
void yyerror(const char *s);
%}


%token NAME STRING TEXT LANGLE RANGLE LANGLE_SLASH EQUALS


%%


xml:
    element { $$ = $1; }
  ;


element:
    LANGLE NAME attributes RANGLE content LANGLE_SLASH NAME RANGLE
{
        if (strcmp($2, $8) != 0) {
            yyerror("Mismatched tag names");
            $$ = create_error_element();
        } else {
            $$ = create_xml_element($2, $3, $5);
```

```
        }
    }
    ;


attributes:
    attributes attribute { $$ = append_attribute($1, $2); }
    | /* empty */ { $$ = create_empty_attribute_list(); }
    ;



attribute:
    NAME EQUALS STRING { $$ = create_xml_attribute($1, $3); }
    ;



content:
    content element { $$ = append_content($1, $2); }
    | content TEXT { $$ = append_text($1, $2); }
    | /* empty */ { $$ = create_empty_content(); }
    ;


%%


void yyerror(const char *s) {
    fprintf(stderr, "XML Parsing error: %s\n", s);
}


int main(void) {
    printf("Enter XML input:\n");
    yyparse();
    // Optionally, traverse and print the XML tree.
    return 0;
}
```

Challenges and Solutions in XML Parsing

Parsing XML with FLEX and YACC highlights several challenges:

- **Handling Mixed Content:** XML elements can contain both child elements and text. The grammar must be designed to handle this interleaving.
- **Tag Matching:** Ensuring that start and end tags match is crucial. Semantic actions must verify tag consistency.
- **Attributes and Escaping:** Attributes may contain special characters that need to be escaped. The lexer and parser must cooperate to process these correctly.

Practical Applications of XML Parsing

While dedicated XML libraries exist, building an XML parser with FLEX and YACC can be a learning tool and can be integrated into custom data processing pipelines. Such a parser might be used for:

- Configuration file processing.
- Lightweight data interchange.
- Educational tools for demonstrating tree-based parsing.

9.5 Implementing a Basic Query Language

Introduction to Query Languages

Query languages, such as SQL, allow users to extract and manipulate data from databases. Although full SQL is complex, implementing a basic query language demonstrates key concepts in parsing command structures, managing lists of conditions, and interfacing with data sources. In this case study, we design a simple query language—"MiniSQL"—that supports basic SELECT statements with WHERE clauses.

Language Features

MiniSQL includes:

- **SELECT Statements:** Queries to retrieve columns from a table.
- **FROM Clause:** Specifying the data source.
- **WHERE Clause:** Allowing filtering conditions using logical operators.
- **Basic Operators:** Equality, inequality, and relational comparisons.

Lexical Analysis for MiniSQL

The FLEX file for MiniSQL (minisql.l) must recognize keywords (SELECT, FROM, WHERE), identifiers (column and table names), numeric literals, strings, and operators.

Token Definitions

In common.h, add tokens for MiniSQL:

```
#ifndef COMMON_H
#define COMMON_H


enum yytokentype {
    NUMBER = 258,
    IDENTIFIER,
    STRING_LITERAL,
```

```
    SELECT,
    FROM,
    WHERE,
    EQUALS,
    NOT_EQUALS,
    LESS_THAN,
    GREATER_THAN,
    AND,
    OR,
    COMMA,
    SEMICOLON,
    // Add tokens as needed.
};


#endif /* COMMON_H */
```

The FLEX Specification

A sample FLEX file might be:

```
%{
#include "common.h"
#include <stdlib.h>
#include <stdio.h>
%}


ID     [a-zA-Z_][a-zA-Z0-9_]*
NUMBER [0-9]+
STRING \'([^\\\']|\\.)*\'


%%


"SELECT"    { return SELECT; }
"FROM"      { return FROM; }
"WHERE"     { return WHERE; }
"AND"       { return AND; }
"OR"        { return OR; }
"="         { return EQUALS; }
"!="        { return NOT_EQUALS; }
"<"         { return LESS_THAN; }
">"         { return GREATER_THAN; }
{NUMBER}    { yylval = atoi(yytext); return NUMBER; }
{STRING}    { yylval = strdup(yytext); return STRING_LITERAL; }
{ID}        { yylval = strdup(yytext); return IDENTIFIER; }
```

```
","        { return COMMA; }
";"        { return SEMICOLON; }
[ \t\n]+    { /* Skip whitespace */ }
.          { printf("Unexpected character: %s\n", yytext); }
%%


int yywrap(void) { return 1; }
```

Grammar and Parsing with YACC

The YACC file for MiniSQL (`minisql.y`) defines the syntax for a simple SELECT query.

Example YACC Specification

```
%{
#include <stdio.h>
#include <stdlib.h>
#include "common.h"
#include "query_ast.h" // Contains definitions for query AST nodes.
void yyerror(const char *s);
%}


%token NUMBER IDENTIFIER STRING_LITERAL SELECT FROM WHERE
EQUALS NOT_EQUALS LESS_THAN GREATER_THAN AND OR COMMA
SEMICOLON


%%


query:
    SELECT select_list FROM table where_clause SEMICOLON { $$ =
create_select_query($2, $4, $5); }
  ;


select_list:
    select_list COMMA IDENTIFIER { $$ = append_column($1, $3); }
  | IDENTIFIER { $$ = create_select_list($1); }
  ;


table:
    IDENTIFIER { $$ = create_table_node($1); }
  ;
```

```
where_clause:
    WHERE condition { $$ = $2; }
  | /* empty */ { $$ = create_empty_condition(); }
  ;


condition:
    condition AND condition { $$ = create_condition_node("AND", $1, $3); }
  | condition OR condition { $$ = create_condition_node("OR", $1, $3); }
  | IDENTIFIER EQUALS value { $$ = create_condition_node("EQUALS", $1,
$3); }
  | IDENTIFIER NOT_EQUALS value { $$ =
create_condition_node("NOT_EQUALS", $1, $3); }
  | IDENTIFIER LESS_THAN value { $$ = create_condition_node("LESS_THAN",
$1, $3); }
  | IDENTIFIER GREATER_THAN value { $$ =
create_condition_node("GREATER_THAN", $1, $3); }
  ;


value:
    NUMBER { $$ = create_value_node(NUMBER, $1); }
  | STRING_LITERAL { $$ = create_value_node(STRING_LITERAL, $1); }
  ;


%%


void yyerror(const char *s) {
    fprintf(stderr, "Query Syntax error: %s\n", s);
}


int main(void) {
    printf("Enter MiniSQL query:\n");
    yyparse();
    // Optionally, process or execute the query.
    return 0;
}
```

Building the AST and Semantic Actions

Semantic actions in the MiniSQL parser build an AST that represents the query. The AST includes nodes for the SELECT list, table references, and conditions in the WHERE clause. These nodes can be traversed later to optimize the query or to translate it into another form (such as an SQL statement for a database engine).

Challenges in Query Language Parsing

Implementing a query language involves unique challenges:

- **Ambiguous Grammar:** Query languages can be ambiguous. Ensuring that keywords are recognized correctly and that the grammar reflects the intended precedence (for example, between AND and OR) is essential.
- **Error Reporting:** When a user inputs an invalid query, the parser must provide clear error messages to help correct the query.
- **Extensibility:** Although MiniSQL is simple, the design should allow for future extension—such as supporting JOIN operations, grouping, or ordering.

Testing and Practical Applications

Test cases for MiniSQL should include queries such as:

- `SELECT name, age FROM employees;`
- `SELECT id FROM products WHERE price > 100 AND stock != 0;`
- Queries with missing clauses or syntax errors to test error recovery.

The MiniSQL case study illustrates how to build a domain-specific query processor that can be integrated into applications such as reporting tools or lightweight databases.

9.6 Lessons Learned and Comparative Analysis

Synthesis of Case Studies

The case studies presented in this chapter—from the simple calculator to MiniLang, JSON, XML, and MiniSQL—demonstrate the versatility of FLEX and YACC. Each project highlights different aspects of language processing:

- **The Simple Calculator:** Focuses on arithmetic evaluation and operator precedence.
- **MiniLang:** Combines variable management, control structures, and scoping to build a small programming language.
- **JSON Parser:** Emphasizes handling nested data formats and building a structured representation for data interchange.
- **XML Parser:** Tackles more complex nested markup and tag matching.
- **MiniSQL:** Illustrates how to parse command languages and build query trees.

Common Challenges Across Projects

Despite their diversity, these projects share common challenges:

- **Ambiguity Resolution:** Every project required careful grammar design to eliminate ambiguities and enforce the intended structure.
- **Error Handling:** Providing meaningful error messages and recovery strategies was critical for all applications.

- **Integration of Semantic Actions:** Embedding semantic actions to build ASTs and perform preliminary semantic checks was a recurring theme.
- **Performance Considerations:** Efficient processing, especially in cases of deeply nested structures (JSON and XML), required attention to recursion and memory management.

Best Practices from the Field

From these case studies, several best practices emerge:

- **Modular Architecture:** Clearly separate the lexer, parser, and semantic analysis stages. Use common headers and interfaces to ensure consistency.
- **Incremental Development:** Start with a minimal working version and extend functionality gradually, testing at each stage.
- **Comprehensive Testing:** Develop unit tests for individual components (lexer, parser, semantic actions) and integration tests for end-to-end functionality.
- **Verbose Debugging:** Utilize debugging modes in FLEX and YACC (e.g., yydebug) and embed logging in semantic actions to trace the processing flow.
- **Error Recovery Mechanisms:** Incorporate error productions and recovery strategies that allow the parser to continue processing and report multiple errors in one run.

Comparative Analysis

Each of the case studies illustrates different strengths of the FLEX and YACC approach:

- **Calculator and MiniLang:** These projects show that even for relatively simple arithmetic or programming languages, the combination of FLEX and YACC is robust and adaptable. The clear separation of lexical and syntactic analysis enables rapid development and debugging.
- **JSON and XML Parsers:** These projects underscore the flexibility of these tools in handling data formats. While JSON is simpler and more linear, XML's nested and mixed content structures present a higher level of complexity that can still be managed with careful grammar design.
- **MiniSQL:** This project demonstrates the capability of FLEX and YACC to parse domain-specific languages that require both command interpretation and complex conditional logic.

The diversity of these projects illustrates that the techniques learned throughout this book are applicable across a wide range of domains, from general-purpose programming languages to specialized data formats and query languages.

9.7 Future Directions and Real-World Implementations

Extending the Case Studies

The projects described here provide a strong foundation, but there are many opportunities for further development:

- **Enhancing MiniLang:** Extend the mini programming language to include functions, arrays, and more sophisticated data types. This could involve adding parameter passing, return types, and more advanced control flow structures.
- **Optimizing Data Parsers:** For JSON and XML, consider adding optimizations such as streaming parsing for large files or incremental parsing for real-time applications.
- **Full-Fledged Query Processors:** Build on MiniSQL to support more complex queries, including JOIN operations, nested queries, and aggregation functions.
- **Integration with Backends:** Combine the frontend with a backend code generator or interpreter to produce executable programs or to process queries directly against a data store.
- **Interactive Development Environments:** Integrate the compilers and parsers into IDEs or web-based interfaces that provide real-time feedback, syntax highlighting, and error diagnostics.

Real-World Case Studies

Numerous real-world systems have been built using similar techniques:

- **Scripting Languages:** Many scripting languages and domain-specific languages use FLEX and YACC (or their modern equivalents) for rapid prototyping and development.
- **Configuration File Parsers:** Tools that parse configuration files (in JSON, XML, or custom formats) often leverage the techniques described here to ensure robustness and flexibility.
- **Database Query Engines:** Lightweight query engines for embedded databases implement similar grammars to MiniSQL, demonstrating that even complex query languages can be parsed using these methods.

Chapter 10: Debugging and Optimization Techniques

In this chapter, we delve into the critical practices of debugging and optimization for compiler frontends built using FLEX and YACC. Unlike previous chapters that concentrated on constructing the various components of a compiler, this chapter is dedicated exclusively to ensuring that these components operate efficiently and correctly under a variety of conditions. Debugging and optimization are integral to the development cycle—they not only improve performance but also significantly enhance the robustness and maintainability of your codebase. In the sections that follow, we will explore detailed strategies, techniques, and tools to identify, diagnose, and resolve issues in your compiler frontend. We will also discuss various optimization approaches—from fine-tuning regular expressions in the lexer to refining grammar rules in the parser and improving memory management across the entire system. Each section is presented in depth to provide a comprehensive guide that is distinct from earlier content.

10.1 Introduction and Overview

Compiler development is a complex and iterative process. Even when a system appears to function correctly on the surface, hidden bugs or inefficiencies may be lurking beneath. Debugging is the process of identifying, isolating, and resolving these issues, while optimization focuses on improving the performance, memory usage, and overall efficiency of the system. Given the multi-phase nature of a compiler frontend—spanning lexical analysis, syntax analysis, semantic processing, symbol table management, and intermediate representation (IR) generation—each phase has its own potential pitfalls and performance bottlenecks.

In this chapter, we begin with an overview of common challenges that arise during debugging and optimization. We then move on to detailed techniques for diagnosing and correcting errors in each component. Whether you are tackling obscure token misclassifications in the lexer, parsing conflicts in YACC, or memory leaks during semantic analysis, the techniques described here will prove invaluable. We will also cover best practices and introduce a range of tools, from built-in debugging modes to external profilers and debuggers, that help automate and streamline the process. Ultimately, the goal is to empower you with a toolkit that enables the creation of reliable, high-performance compiler frontends.

10.2 Debugging Techniques in Compiler Frontends

Debugging a compiler frontend involves tackling issues that may emerge in multiple layers. Each phase of the compiler—lexical, syntactic, semantic, and IR generation—has its own set of challenges. In this section, we discuss various debugging techniques that address problems specific to each phase, along with methods to debug cross-cutting issues such as memory management and performance bottlenecks.

10.2.1 Debugging Lexical Analysis with FLEX

The lexical analyzer (lexer) is the first component to process source code. It uses regular expressions to match patterns and produce tokens. Even small errors in the lexer can lead to cascading failures in later stages. Here are several strategies to debug the lexer effectively:

- **Verbose Logging in Actions:** Embedding print statements within lexical rules is one of the simplest yet most effective techniques. For example, when a rule matches a numeric literal, logging the matched string and its converted value can help verify that the lexer is processing input as expected.

  Example:

  ```
  {NUMBER} {
      double val = atof(yytext);
      printf("DEBUG: Matched NUMBER '%s' -> %lf\n", yytext, val);
      yylval = val;
      return NUMBER;
  }
  ```

  Such logs are invaluable when troubleshooting issues like incorrect token conversion or unexpected token types.

- **Using Test Cases for the Lexer:** Create a suite of test cases specifically for the lexer. Run your lexer on various inputs—both typical and edge-case scenarios—to ensure that every pattern behaves correctly. Automated scripts that compare expected outputs with actual results can streamline this process.
- **Interactive Debugging Tools:** While FLEX does not provide a built-in debugger, you can compile the generated lexer with debugging symbols (using -g in GCC) and use tools like GDB. Setting breakpoints in key functions (e.g., yywrap() or within the generated yylex() function) allows you to step through the code and inspect internal states.

- **Regular Expression Analysis:** Evaluate your regular expressions for efficiency and correctness. Tools that simulate regular expression matching or analyze their complexity can be helpful. Ensuring that your patterns do not lead to catastrophic backtracking is essential, especially when processing large inputs.
- **Error Handling in the Lexer:** Implement robust error reporting for unrecognized characters or malformed tokens. Logging unexpected characters with context (such as line numbers and surrounding text) can help identify issues early.

10.2.2 Debugging Syntax Analysis with YACC

YACC generates a parser that constructs a parse tree or abstract syntax tree (AST) based on the grammar you provide. Debugging the parser involves identifying issues such as shift/reduce conflicts, incorrect tree construction, or unexpected behavior during error recovery.

- **Enabling YACC Debug Mode:** YACC offers a built-in debugging option through the global variable yydebug. By setting yydebug = 1 in your main() function, you can observe detailed trace information about state transitions, token shifts, and reductions. This verbose output is critical for understanding how the parser processes the input.

   Example:

```
int main(void) {
    yydebug = 1;
    yyparse();
    return 0;
}
```

- **Analyzing Conflict Reports:** When YACC generates conflicts (shift/reduce or reduce/reduce), it produces a report (often in a file like y.output). Study this report carefully to understand where ambiguities exist in your grammar. Sometimes, adjusting operator precedence or refactoring grammar rules can resolve these conflicts.
- **Instrumentation in Semantic Actions:** Insert print statements within your semantic actions to output the values being computed and the AST nodes being constructed. For instance, logging the creation of an operator node along with its operands can help verify that the tree structure matches expectations.
- **Visualizing the Parse Tree:** Although YACC does not inherently provide tree visualization, you can write functions to traverse and print the AST. Visual representations often make it easier to spot structural issues that textual debug output might obscure.
- **Unit Testing Individual Productions:** Write unit tests that feed the parser with isolated productions. For example, test the parsing of arithmetic expressions independently to ensure that operator precedence is respected and that parentheses are handled correctly.

10.2.3 Debugging Semantic Actions and Type Checking

Semantic actions are where the parser bridges the gap between syntax and meaning. They are responsible for constructing the AST, performing type checking, and enforcing language semantics.

- **Logging Semantic Values:** As with lexical debugging, log the semantic values computed in each action. This includes intermediate values in arithmetic expressions, type information in assignments, and any error flags set during processing.

Example:

```
expression:
    expression PLUS expression {
        printf("DEBUG: Adding %lf and %lf\n", $1, $3);
        $$ = $1 + $3;
    }
```

- **Using Assertions:** Incorporate assertions in your semantic actions to validate assumptions. For example, assert that pointers to AST nodes are not NULL before accessing their fields. Assertions can catch inconsistencies early in the execution flow.
- **Type Checking and Error Reporting:** Ensure that your semantic actions for type checking provide detailed error messages. When a type mismatch is detected, report not only that an error occurred but also include the expected type, the actual type, and the source location. This level of detail is critical when debugging complex language features.
- **Modularizing Complex Actions:** For complex semantic processing, delegate tasks to helper functions. Debug these functions independently, and log their inputs and outputs to ensure they behave as expected. Modularization reduces the cognitive load when diagnosing errors in large semantic actions.

10.2.4 Debugging Memory Management and Symbol Tables

Memory management issues, such as leaks or invalid accesses, are particularly challenging in compiler construction due to dynamic allocations in the lexer, parser, and semantic actions.

- **Valgrind and Memory Profilers:** Use tools like Valgrind to detect memory leaks and invalid memory accesses. Run your compiler frontend under Valgrind's supervision to catch errors that might not be apparent through normal testing.
- **Consistent Use of Memory Pools:** When managing large numbers of small allocations (e.g., AST nodes or symbol table entries), consider using a memory pool or arena allocator. This not only improves performance but also makes it easier to free memory in bulk when a scope is exited.
- **Logging Allocations and Deallocations:** Implement logging in your memory management routines to trace every allocation and deallocation. This helps identify mismatches and pinpoint where leaks might be occurring.

- **Debugging the Symbol Table:** Since the symbol table is a critical component, incorporate functions that can print the current state of the symbol table at key points (e.g., when entering or exiting a scope). Visualizing the symbol table can reveal issues like duplicate entries or incorrect scope handling.

10.3 Tools and Methods for Effective Debugging

Beyond built-in debugging techniques, there is a range of external tools and methods that can significantly aid in the debugging process.

10.3.1 GDB: The GNU Debugger

GDB is an essential tool for debugging C programs and, by extension, the C code generated by FLEX and YACC.

- **Setting Breakpoints:** Use breakpoints in critical functions such as `yylex()`, `yyparse()`, and within your semantic action helper functions. This allows you to pause execution at points of interest and inspect variable states.
- **Stepping Through Code:** Step through your code line by line to understand the flow of execution. This is especially useful in deeply recursive parsing routines where the control flow may be non-obvious.
- **Inspecting Memory and Variables:** Use commands like `print` and `info locals` to examine the values of variables and memory contents. This is particularly useful when diagnosing issues in AST construction or symbol table management.

10.3.2 Valgrind: Detecting Memory Issues

Valgrind is a dynamic analysis tool that can detect memory leaks, buffer overflows, and invalid memory accesses.

- **Leak Checks:** Run your compiler frontend under Valgrind to identify memory leaks. Addressing leaks early can prevent performance degradation and stability issues in long-running applications.
- **Detailed Error Reports:** Valgrind provides detailed reports on where invalid accesses occur. Use this information to trace back to the offending code in your lexer, parser, or semantic actions.
- **Integrating with Continuous Integration:** Incorporate Valgrind checks into your CI/CD pipeline to catch memory issues as soon as new code is integrated.

10.3.3 Profiling Tools for Performance Optimization

Performance profiling is key to identifying bottlenecks in your compiler frontend. Several tools are available:

- **Gprof:** Gprof can profile your application to identify functions that consume the most execution time. Use it to optimize critical sections, such as complex semantic actions or deep recursion in the parser.

- **Perf:** Perf is a powerful Linux profiling tool that provides insights into CPU and memory usage. It can help identify system-level performance issues that might not be apparent from source-level analysis.
- **Custom Instrumentation:** Consider adding custom instrumentation—such as timing functions or counters—in key parts of your code. This can be particularly useful for measuring the impact of specific optimizations.

10.3.4 Logging Libraries and Instrumentation

While simple `printf` statements are useful, a logging library offers more control and flexibility.

- **Log Levels:** Use log levels (DEBUG, INFO, WARNING, ERROR) to control the verbosity of your output. During development, set the log level to DEBUG; in production, reduce it to WARNING or ERROR.
- **Timestamping and Context:** Ensure that each log entry includes a timestamp and contextual information, such as the function name and line number. This contextual information is invaluable when diagnosing issues over long execution periods.
- **Rotating Log Files:** For long-running compiler processes or integration into larger systems, implement log rotation to manage file sizes and archival.

10.4 Optimization Techniques

Optimization is a continuous process aimed at improving performance, reducing resource consumption, and enhancing the overall efficiency of your compiler frontend. This section outlines optimization strategies across different components of the system.

10.4.1 Lexical Analysis Optimization

Optimizing the lexer involves refining regular expressions and ensuring that the pattern-matching process is as efficient as possible.

- **Efficient Regular Expressions:** Simplify regular expressions where possible to reduce processing overhead. Avoid overly complex patterns that could lead to excessive backtracking.
- **Buffering and Input Handling:** FLEX uses internal buffering to manage input. Tuning buffer sizes can improve performance, especially when processing large files. Consider increasing the buffer size if your inputs are very large.
- **Minimizing Actions:** Keep the code in each action as lean as possible. Move complex computations or function calls to helper routines that can be optimized separately.
- **Inlining Critical Actions:** For frequently matched tokens, consider inlining the associated actions to reduce function call overhead.

10.4.2 Parser Optimization

The parser, generated by YACC, can be optimized by refining the grammar and minimizing the overhead in semantic actions.

- **Grammar Simplification:** Remove unnecessary productions and refactor ambiguous rules to minimize conflicts. A simplified grammar often results in a smaller parse table and faster parsing times.
- **Precedence and Associativity Declarations:** Use precedence and associativity declarations to resolve conflicts efficiently. This reduces the computational cost of disambiguating expressions during parsing.
- **Optimizing Semantic Actions:** Reduce the complexity of semantic actions by modularizing the code. Avoid redundant computations by caching results when possible.
- **Tail Recursion Optimization:** Where applicable, write productions in a tail-recursive manner. This can help some compilers optimize recursion into iteration, reducing the stack usage.

10.4.3 Semantic and IR Generation Optimization

Optimizing semantic actions and IR generation can lead to significant performance improvements in later stages of the compiler.

- **Constant Folding:** Integrate constant folding directly into semantic actions to evaluate constant expressions at compile time. This reduces the workload during execution.
- **Dead Code Elimination:** Implement mechanisms to identify and eliminate dead code within semantic actions. This involves detecting unreachable branches or redundant computations.
- **Efficient IR Construction:** Design your intermediate representation (IR) to be simple and easy to traverse. Use data structures that allow for rapid insertion, deletion, and iteration.
- **Reusing Computed Values:** Cache frequently used intermediate results to avoid recalculating them. This is particularly important in the generation of IR where many similar operations occur.

10.4.4 Memory Management and Resource Optimization

Memory management is a common source of inefficiency in compiler frontends. Optimizing memory usage not only speeds up execution but also reduces the risk of leaks and crashes.

- **Memory Pooling:** Use memory pools to allocate small objects (like AST nodes or symbol table entries). Memory pooling reduces the overhead of individual malloc/free calls and can improve cache performance.
- **Efficient Data Structures:** Choose data structures that balance speed and memory usage. For example, using hash tables for the symbol table can provide fast lookups while controlling memory overhead.

- **Garbage Collection:** Although manual memory management is common in C, consider implementing simple garbage collection strategies for temporary objects created during parsing.
- **Profiling Memory Usage:** Use tools like Valgrind and custom instrumentation to monitor memory usage and identify leaks. Refactor code based on profiling results to eliminate inefficiencies.

10.4.5 Compiler Frontend Pipeline Optimization

The overall pipeline—from lexical analysis through IR generation—can be optimized by ensuring that data flows smoothly between components.

- **Minimizing Data Copies:** Avoid unnecessary copying of data between the lexer, parser, and semantic actions. Use pointers and references where appropriate.
- **Efficient Interfaces:** Define clear, lightweight interfaces between the different compiler components. This reduces the overhead of transitioning from one phase to another.
- **Parallelizing Independent Tasks:** Although compiler frontends are traditionally sequential, some tasks (like lexing and preliminary parsing of independent modules) can be parallelized to take advantage of multi-core processors.

10.4.6 Profiling and Continuous Optimization

Optimization is an ongoing process that requires regular profiling and testing.

- **Benchmarking:** Create benchmarks for your compiler frontend using a variety of input sizes and complexities. Measure metrics such as processing time, memory usage, and throughput.
- **Profiling Tools:** Use gprof, perf, or similar profiling tools to identify hotspots in your code. Focus optimization efforts on functions or sections that consume the most resources.
- **Regression Testing:** Maintain a robust regression test suite to ensure that optimizations do not break existing functionality. Continuous integration tools can run these tests automatically after each change.
- **Iterative Optimization:** Optimization should be iterative. Implement changes, measure their impact, and refine further. Document changes and their effects to guide future efforts.

10.5 Best Practices for Debugging and Optimization

Combining robust debugging techniques with systematic optimization practices is key to developing a high-quality compiler frontend. In this section, we summarize the best practices that emerge from our discussion.

10.5.1 Adopt a Modular Architecture

- **Separation of Concerns:** Ensure that the lexer, parser, semantic analyzer, symbol table, and IR generator are implemented as independent modules. This modularity makes it easier to isolate and fix bugs as well as optimize individual components.
- **Clear Interfaces:** Define clear, consistent interfaces between modules. Use shared header files for token definitions, semantic value types, and common data structures to avoid inconsistencies.

10.5.2 Implement Comprehensive Logging and Instrumentation

- **Logging Strategy:** Use a logging library that supports multiple log levels (DEBUG, INFO, WARN, ERROR) to control output verbosity. Log critical events, such as token matches, parser reductions, and memory allocations.
- **Instrumentation:** Add instrumentation code to measure execution time and memory usage in critical sections. Use timestamps and counters to capture performance metrics that can guide optimization efforts.

10.5.3 Embrace Automated Testing and Continuous Integration

- **Unit Testing:** Develop unit tests for individual modules. For example, test the lexer on a range of input strings, and verify that the parser produces the expected AST for given expressions.
- **Integration Testing:** Create integration tests that cover the entire compilation process—from source code input to IR generation. Include both valid and invalid inputs to test error recovery.
- **Regression Testing:** Maintain a suite of regression tests to ensure that new optimizations or debugging changes do not introduce new bugs. Integrate these tests into a CI/CD pipeline.

10.5.4 Profile Regularly and Optimize Iteratively

- **Frequent Profiling:** Regularly profile your system during development. Use tools like GDB, Valgrind, and perf to monitor performance and memory usage. Identify hotspots and prioritize optimization in those areas.
- **Iterative Refinement:** Apply optimization changes incrementally. Measure the impact of each change to ensure that it delivers the desired improvements without unintended side effects.
- **Documentation:** Document all optimizations and debugging strategies. Keeping detailed records of performance improvements helps guide future development and troubleshooting.

10.5.5 Practice Defensive Programming

- **Assertions and Validations:** Use assertions liberally to catch unexpected conditions early in the code. Validate inputs to functions, especially in semantic actions and symbol table routines.

- **Robust Error Handling:** Implement robust error handling in every module. Ensure that errors in one phase (e.g., lexical analysis) are gracefully propagated to the next phase (e.g., parsing) without causing a system-wide failure.
- **Memory Safety:** Follow best practices in memory management. Use memory pools, check for NULL pointers, and ensure that every allocation is paired with a deallocation.

10.6 Case Studies in Debugging and Optimization

Real-world examples provide invaluable insights into the debugging and optimization process. In this section, we describe several case studies drawn from practical experiences that illustrate common pitfalls and effective solutions.

10.6.1 Case Study: Optimizing a Complex Expression Parser

A compiler frontend for a domain-specific language included a complex expression parser that suffered from slow performance on deeply nested expressions. The debugging process revealed that excessive recursion and redundant semantic actions were the primary culprits. The solution involved:

- Refactoring the grammar to use tail recursion where possible.
- Caching the results of frequently computed sub-expressions.
- Streamlining the semantic actions to reduce unnecessary function calls.

Profiling with gprof showed a 40% reduction in processing time after these optimizations, validating the changes.

10.6.2 Case Study: Resolving Memory Leaks in a Symbol Table Module

In another project, extensive testing under Valgrind uncovered subtle memory leaks in the symbol table. The leaks were traced to improper deallocation of dynamically allocated identifier strings when exiting a scope. The debugging process involved:

- Adding logging to the symbol table insertion and deletion functions.
- Modifying the scope exit routine to iterate over all entries and free associated memory.
- Introducing memory pooling to reduce allocation overhead.

After these changes, repeated test runs under Valgrind showed no memory leaks, and overall memory usage dropped significantly.

10.6.3 Case Study: Debugging an XML Parser

An XML parser built with FLEX and YACC was intermittently failing to correctly match start and end tags. Debugging this issue required:

- Enabling YACC's debugging mode to trace the parser's state transitions.
- Instrumenting semantic actions to log the tag names as they were processed.

- Identifying a subtle bug in the lexer where the regular expression for names allowed trailing whitespace.
- Refining the lexer pattern and adding a trim function to remove extraneous spaces.

These changes resulted in the parser correctly matching tags even in complex, nested XML documents.

10.6.4 Case Study: Performance Tuning a JSON Parser

A JSON parser intended for high-volume data processing was found to have performance issues during large-scale testing. Profiling revealed that:

- The regular expressions used in the lexer were overly complex, causing significant backtracking.
- The AST construction in the parser was creating many small allocations.
- The error recovery paths were not optimized, leading to unnecessary processing delays on encountering malformed input.

The optimizations included:

- Simplifying regular expressions and pre-compiling frequently used patterns.
- Implementing a memory pool for AST nodes.
- Optimizing error recovery routines by adding early exits in the case of minor errors.

Subsequent benchmarks indicated a 50% improvement in throughput.

10.7 Future Directions and Advanced Strategies

While the techniques discussed so far provide a strong foundation for debugging and optimization, the field of compiler construction is continuously evolving. Here we discuss some advanced strategies and future directions that can further enhance your compiler frontend.

10.7.1 Advanced Static Analysis

Incorporate advanced static analysis techniques into your compiler frontend to catch potential issues before runtime. Techniques such as data-flow analysis, control-flow analysis, and type inference can be integrated into the semantic phase to identify dead code, optimize variable usage, and improve overall program efficiency.

10.7.2 Machine Learning for Error Prediction

Emerging research in applying machine learning to compiler error detection shows promise. By training models on historical error data, it is possible to predict and even automatically correct common mistakes. Future compiler frontends may integrate such predictive models to offer real-time suggestions and error corrections.

10.7.3 Dynamic Optimization and JIT Compilation

For high-performance applications, consider integrating just-in-time (JIT) compilation techniques. JIT compilers dynamically optimize code at runtime, based on profiling data. Although this extends beyond traditional compiler frontends, incorporating a feedback loop that passes profiling information back into the IR generation phase can lead to significant performance gains.

10.7.4 Parallel and Distributed Compilation

Modern processors and distributed systems offer opportunities to parallelize compilation tasks. Explore techniques to divide the input into independent modules that can be processed concurrently. This involves not only parallelizing lexical analysis and parsing but also ensuring that symbol tables and IR generation can be safely shared or merged.

10.7.5 Integration with Modern Development Environments

As compilers become integral to integrated development environments (IDEs), consider how debugging and optimization techniques can be extended to support interactive development. Real-time error highlighting, incremental parsing, and live performance metrics are features that can enhance the developer experience.

10.8 Concluding Thoughts on Debugging and Optimization

Effective debugging and optimization are not one-time tasks—they are integral to the entire development lifecycle of a compiler frontend. The strategies discussed in this chapter have shown that by employing systematic logging, using powerful tools like GDB and Valgrind, and continuously profiling performance, you can build robust, efficient systems that stand up to the rigors of real-world applications. Moreover, iterative improvements, thorough testing, and a modular design ensure that your code remains maintainable and extensible as the project grows.

Debugging often reveals the hidden complexities of a system. Whether it is a subtle error in a regular expression or a deep-seated memory leak in the symbol table, the process of debugging forces a deeper understanding of the system's internals. Optimization, on the other hand, is an ongoing effort to make the system not only correct but also efficient. The case studies presented illustrate that even minor tweaks can yield significant performance improvements. As you continue to refine your compiler frontend, these practices will be indispensable tools in your development arsenal.

Looking to the future, the integration of advanced static analysis, machine learning, and dynamic optimization techniques holds promise for even more intelligent and adaptive compilers. The foundation laid by traditional tools like FLEX and YACC remains relevant, but modern challenges require a continual evolution of debugging and optimization strategies.

Chapter 11: Beyond FLEX and YACC – Modern Alternatives

The world of language processing and compiler construction has evolved significantly since the days when FLEX and YACC were the dominant tools for building compilers. While FLEX and YACC have been invaluable in teaching and prototyping, modern software development demands greater flexibility, improved error reporting, enhanced performance, and easier integration with contemporary development environments. In this chapter, we explore the modern alternatives to FLEX and YACC, examining a variety of parser generators and language workbenches that have emerged over the years. We will discuss their underlying technologies, advantages and limitations, and provide insights into how they address many of the challenges inherent in traditional approaches. We will also delve into real-world case studies and emerging trends in parsing technology.

11.1 Introduction and Motivation

The Limitations of Traditional Tools

FLEX and YACC revolutionized compiler construction by automating the tedious process of writing lexical analyzers and parsers. Their strengths lie in their simplicity, close integration with C, and a rich history in academic settings. However, several limitations have become evident over time:

- **Complex Error Handling:** FLEX and YACC generate error messages that can be cryptic. The error recovery mechanisms often require manual tweaking, and the debugging output does not always provide the context modern developers need.
- **Limited Language Support:** The generated code is tightly coupled with C, making integration with modern languages (such as Java, C#, or even Python) less straightforward.

- **Maintenance Difficulties:** As languages evolve, the rigid structure of traditional lex/yacc tools can hinder rapid prototyping. Grammar modifications often require careful reworking to resolve conflicts, and managing large grammars can be cumbersome.
- **Scalability Issues:** For large-scale language projects, the performance and memory usage of the generated parsers may become problematic. Additionally, integrating with modern IDEs and debugging tools is not always seamless.

Why Modern Alternatives?

The demand for more expressive, maintainable, and powerful parser generators has led to the development of modern alternatives that address these limitations. These tools offer several benefits:

- **Improved Error Reporting and Recovery:** Modern parser generators provide more detailed error messages, context-aware recovery mechanisms, and support for interactive debugging.
- **Enhanced Language Integration:** Many modern tools generate code in multiple programming languages or offer bindings to high-level languages, making it easier to integrate the parser with contemporary software ecosystems.
- **Better Performance and Scalability:** Newer algorithms and data structures have led to parsers that are more efficient in terms of both speed and memory usage. They can handle large, complex grammars with ease.
- **Developer-Friendly Features:** Tools with visual grammar editors, integrated testing frameworks, and robust documentation help reduce the learning curve and improve productivity.

Overview of Modern Alternatives

This chapter will explore several modern alternatives to FLEX and YACC, categorized into different families:

- **Modern Parser Generators:** Tools such as ANTLR, Bison (an evolution of YACC), and Lemon provide a more modern approach while retaining familiar concepts.
- **Parsing Expression Grammars (PEG):** Parser generators based on PEGs (e.g., PEG.js, Rats!) offer an alternative formalism that eliminates many ambiguities inherent in context-free grammars.
- **Combinator Parsing Libraries:** In functional languages like Haskell or Scala, parser combinator libraries allow the construction of parsers by composing small functions, yielding highly readable and maintainable code.
- **Tree-Sitter:** A relatively new tool that has gained traction for building fast, incremental parsers for programming languages, often used in modern IDEs.
- **Language Workbenches and DSL Frameworks:** Tools such as JetBrains MPS or Xtext provide integrated environments for language design, offering advanced features like projectional editing and domain-specific language (DSL) development.

In the following sections, we examine these alternatives in detail, comparing their features, discussing their use cases, and considering how they can be integrated into modern development workflows.

11.2 Modern Parser Generators

Modern parser generators build on the principles of traditional tools but incorporate new algorithms, better error handling, and improved integration with current programming languages. Here, we discuss several widely used modern parser generators.

11.2.1 ANTLR (Another Tool for Language Recognition)

Overview

ANTLR is perhaps one of the most popular modern parser generators. It is designed to build both lexers and parsers and supports multiple target languages, including Java, C#, Python, JavaScript, and more. ANTLR uses a grammar notation that is both powerful and human-readable, and its generated parsers are recursive-descent parsers that can handle complex language constructs.

Key Features

- **Integrated Lexer and Parser:** ANTLR uses a unified grammar file to define both the lexical and syntactic structure of a language, reducing the need to maintain separate files.
- **Rich Error Reporting:** ANTLR provides built-in error handling that generates informative messages, making it easier to diagnose and fix issues.
- **Multiple Target Languages:** The ability to generate parsers in various languages means that ANTLR can be integrated into a wide range of projects.
- **Tooling and IDE Support:** ANTLRWorks, an IDE for developing ANTLR grammars, offers features such as syntax highlighting, grammar debugging, and visualization of parse trees.

Example Use Cases

ANTLR is widely used for building programming language compilers, interpreters, and even natural language processing tools. Its flexibility makes it suitable for both academic research and industrial applications.

Advantages and Limitations

- **Advantages:**
    - Highly expressive grammar syntax
    - Comprehensive error handling and recovery
    - Strong community support and extensive documentation
- **Limitations:**
    - The learning curve can be steep for beginners due to its advanced features

- o Recursive-descent parsers may have performance issues with certain types of left recursion, although ANTLR provides mechanisms to mitigate this

11.2.2 Bison

Overview

GNU Bison is a modern replacement for YACC. It retains the fundamental approach of generating parsers from context-free grammars but incorporates numerous enhancements, including improved error messages, additional language constructs, and better compatibility with modern C and C++ standards.

Key Features

- **Enhanced Compatibility:** Bison supports a wider range of C/C++ features and integrates more smoothly with contemporary development environments.
- **Improved Diagnostics:** The error messages produced by Bison are more detailed than those from traditional YACC, aiding in debugging and grammar refinement.
- **Support for GLR Parsing:** Bison offers a Generalized LR parser, which can handle ambiguous grammars more gracefully than standard LR parsers.

Example Use Cases

Bison is used in many open-source projects and has a long history in the Unix world. It is ideal for projects that require the robustness of traditional LR parsing but with modern enhancements.

Advantages and Limitations

- **Advantages:**
  - o Familiar to developers with a YACC background
  - o Extensive documentation and proven track record
  - o Enhanced support for C/C++ and GLR parsing
- **Limitations:**
  - o Still inherently tied to C/C++ environments
  - o Some features may be overkill for small or simple projects

11.2.3 Lemon

Overview

Lemon is a parser generator that takes a different approach compared to YACC and Bison. It produces parsers in C and is known for its simplicity and efficiency. Lemon's design emphasizes clarity and small code size, making it suitable for embedded systems and projects where resources are constrained.

Key Features

- **Simplicity and Clarity:** The grammar specification in Lemon is concise and easy to understand, making it a good choice for simpler projects.
- **Deterministic Behavior:** Lemon is designed to produce deterministic parsers that are easy to debug.
- **Lightweight:** The generated parsers are small in size and have low overhead, making Lemon ideal for resource-constrained environments.

Example Use Cases

Lemon has been used in embedded systems and applications where memory and processing power are limited. Its straightforward approach makes it an excellent tool for educational purposes as well.

Advantages and Limitations

- **Advantages:**
  - Very lightweight and efficient
  - Easy to integrate with C projects
  - Deterministic and easy to debug
- **Limitations:**
  - Limited to C, which may restrict integration with other languages
  - Lacks some of the advanced features of more modern tools like ANTLR

11.3 Parsing Expression Grammars (PEG) and Related Tools

Parsing Expression Grammars (PEG) offer an alternative to the context-free grammars used by FLEX and YACC. PEGs provide a different formalism that eliminates ambiguity by design, using prioritized choice rather than nondeterministic rules. Several modern parser generators are based on PEGs.

11.3.1 PEG.js

Overview

PEG.js is a popular parser generator for JavaScript that uses Parsing Expression Grammars. It allows developers to write grammars in a clean, concise syntax and generates a parser that can be used directly in web applications or Node.js environments.

Key Features

- **Unambiguous Grammars:** PEGs do not suffer from the ambiguity issues common in context-free grammars because they use ordered choices to resolve conflicts.
- **JavaScript Integration:** Since PEG.js generates parsers in JavaScript, it integrates seamlessly with modern web development.

- **Readable Grammar Syntax:** The grammar definitions in PEG.js are easy to read and write, making it accessible to developers with varying levels of expertise.

Example Use Cases

PEG.js is widely used in web applications for parsing configuration files, DSLs, and even parts of natural language. Its integration with JavaScript makes it a natural choice for front-end and back-end web development.

Advantages and Limitations

- **Advantages:**
    - ○ Eliminates grammar ambiguity through ordered choices
    - ○ Easy to integrate with web technologies
    - ○ Supports incremental parsing and interactive development
- **Limitations:**
    - ○ Performance may vary depending on the complexity of the grammar
    - ○ Debugging can be challenging if the grammar is not carefully designed

11.3.2 Rats!

Overview

Rats! is another parser generator that uses PEGs, targeting languages like C. It emphasizes simplicity and clarity in grammar definitions while providing the benefits of unambiguous parsing.

Key Features

- **PEG-Based Formalism:** Like PEG.js, Rats! uses Parsing Expression Grammars, ensuring that the generated parser is deterministic and free from ambiguities inherent in traditional CFG-based systems.
- **C Code Generation:** Rats! generates parsers in C, making it suitable for projects that need to integrate with legacy C code or require high performance.
- **Readable and Maintainable Grammars:** The grammar syntax in Rats! is designed to be both expressive and maintainable, which aids in long-term project management.

Example Use Cases

Rats! is often used in projects where performance is critical, and the target environment is C-based. It is also useful in academic settings to demonstrate the advantages of PEGs over traditional grammar systems.

Advantages and Limitations

- **Advantages:**
    - ○ Unambiguous parsing ensures consistent behavior
    - ○ High performance due to C integration

   o   Clear and maintainable grammar syntax
- **Limitations:**
  - o   Limited support for languages other than C
  - o   Smaller community and less extensive documentation compared to ANTLR

11.4 Combinator Parsing Libraries

In functional programming languages such as Haskell, Scala, and OCaml, parser combinator libraries offer an elegant alternative to traditional parser generators. These libraries allow developers to build parsers by composing small, reusable functions.

11.4.1 Parsec (Haskell)

Overview

Parsec is a widely used parser combinator library in Haskell. It allows developers to write highly expressive parsers that are modular and easy to reason about. Because Haskell's functional paradigm encourages composition, Parsec parsers are often more concise than their YACC-based counterparts.

Key Features

- **High-Level Abstractions:** Parsec provides combinators for common parsing patterns, making it easier to construct complex parsers from simpler ones.
- **Error Reporting:** Parsec is known for its excellent error messages, which include detailed information about the expected input and the point of failure.
- **Modularity:** The composability of Parsec parsers allows for rapid development and testing of individual components.

Example Use Cases

Parsec is used extensively in academic research, as well as in production systems that require the robust parsing of complex input. Its ability to handle recursive patterns and context-sensitive constructs makes it ideal for building DSLs and configuration file parsers.

Advantages and Limitations

- **Advantages:**
  - o   Extremely expressive and modular
  - o   Excellent error messages
  - o   Leverages Haskell's strong type system for added safety
- **Limitations:**
  - o   Requires familiarity with functional programming paradigms
  - o   May not be suitable for projects that need to integrate with imperative languages

11.4.2 Scala Parser Combinators

Overview

Scala's parser combinator library is another powerful tool for building parsers. It allows developers to define grammars directly in Scala code, taking advantage of Scala's concise syntax and functional features.

Key Features

- **Seamless Integration with Scala:** Being a part of the Scala ecosystem, the parser combinators integrate naturally with other Scala libraries and frameworks.
- **Expressive Syntax:** The combinator approach leads to highly readable and maintainable grammar definitions.
- **Functional and Imperative Support:** Scala's hybrid nature means that parser combinators can be used in both functional and imperative styles, offering flexibility in design.

Example Use Cases

Scala parser combinators have been used to build compilers, interpreters, and DSLs in the Scala community. They are particularly well-suited for projects that require rapid prototyping and interactive parsing capabilities.

Advantages and Limitations

- **Advantages:**
  - High expressiveness and readability
  - Direct integration with the Scala language
  - Flexibility in handling both functional and imperative code
- **Limitations:**
  - Performance may be a concern for very large inputs
  - The approach may not translate directly to non-Scala environments

11.5 Tree-Sitter and Incremental Parsing

Tree-Sitter is a modern parsing library that has gained popularity for its ability to perform incremental parsing. Originally developed to power code analysis and syntax highlighting in modern text editors, Tree-Sitter offers features that are particularly useful in interactive development environments.

11.5.1 Overview of Tree-Sitter

Tree-Sitter is designed to generate parsers that are both fast and incremental, meaning they can update the parse tree in response to small changes in the source code without re-parsing the entire file. This is invaluable for applications such as IDEs, where responsiveness is critical.

- **Incremental Parsing:** Tree-Sitter updates only the portions of the parse tree that have changed, leading to significant performance improvements in interactive environments.
- **Rich API:** It provides a robust API for querying and traversing the parse tree, which can be used for syntax highlighting, code navigation, and static analysis.
- **Language Agnostic:** Although Tree-Sitter requires a grammar definition, it supports a wide range of languages and can be integrated with various programming environments.

Example Use Cases

Tree-Sitter is used by popular editors such as Atom and Neovim to provide real-time syntax highlighting and code navigation. It is also employed in tools that require efficient parsing of large codebases.

Advantages and Limitations

- **Advantages:**
  - Incremental parsing leads to high performance in dynamic environments
  - Rich and flexible API for code analysis
  - Actively maintained and rapidly evolving community
- **Limitations:**
  - The grammar definition process can be more involved than traditional parser generators
  - May not be ideal for batch processing of static files where incremental updates are unnecessary

11.6 Language Workbenches and DSL Frameworks

Language workbenches provide an integrated environment for designing, implementing, and testing domain-specific languages (DSLs). They often combine grammar editing, parser generation, and IDE integration into a single package.

11.6.1 JetBrains MPS (Meta Programming System)

Overview

JetBrains MPS is a language workbench that takes a unique approach by using projectional editing instead of traditional text-based parsing. This allows for the creation of DSLs that do not rely on parsing ambiguities because the language is directly represented as an abstract syntax tree.

Key Features

- **Projectional Editing:** Users interact with the language through a structured editor that directly manipulates the AST, eliminating many parsing errors.

- **Rich Language Definition:** MPS allows you to define both the syntax and semantics of a language, along with code generation templates.
- **Integrated Development Environment:** The workbench provides tools for debugging, refactoring, and testing, making it a comprehensive solution for DSL development.

Example Use Cases

MPS is used for developing internal DSLs in large organizations, where custom languages are needed to solve domain-specific problems. Its projectional editing approach is particularly beneficial for languages with complex or non-linear syntax.

Advantages and Limitations

- **Advantages:**
  - Eliminates parsing ambiguities through direct AST manipulation
  - Provides a fully integrated development environment for DSLs
  - Highly customizable and extensible
- **Limitations:**
  - Steeper learning curve compared to traditional parser generators
  - The projectional editing paradigm can be unfamiliar to users accustomed to text-based editors

11.6.2 Xtext

Overview

Xtext is an open-source framework for developing DSLs, primarily targeting the Java ecosystem. It integrates grammar definition, parser generation, and IDE support, and it leverages Eclipse as its primary development environment.

Key Features

- **Unified Grammar Definition:** Xtext uses a single grammar file to define the structure of the DSL, generate a parser, and produce an editor with features like syntax highlighting and auto-completion.
- **Integration with Eclipse:** The generated editors are fully integrated into Eclipse, providing a seamless experience for developers.
- **Rich Semantic Support:** Xtext supports advanced features such as scoping, linking, and validation out of the box, which are critical for complex DSLs.

Example Use Cases

Xtext is used extensively in academic projects and industrial settings where DSLs are needed for configuration, modeling, or domain-specific programming. Its tight integration with the Eclipse ecosystem makes it a popular choice for Java-based projects.

Advantages and Limitations

- **Advantages:**
  - ○ Comprehensive support for DSL development
  - ○ Strong integration with modern IDEs
  - ○ Extensive documentation and community support
- **Limitations:**
  - ○ Primarily targeted at the Java ecosystem, which may limit its use in other environments
  - ○ The framework can be heavyweight for simple languages

11.7 Comparative Analysis of Modern Alternatives

When evaluating modern alternatives to FLEX and YACC, several criteria come into play:

11.7.1 Ease of Use and Learning Curve

- **ANTLR:** Offers a rich set of features with a moderate learning curve; ideal for users with some background in compiler construction.
- **Bison/Lemon:** More familiar to those with a YACC background, but may require significant changes to adopt modern practices.
- **PEG-Based Tools (PEG.js, Rats!):** Generally easier to understand due to unambiguous grammar definitions; however, the ordered choice semantics require careful planning.
- **Parser Combinators (Parsec, Scala Parser Combinators):** Extremely expressive and modular, but require comfort with functional programming paradigms.
- **Tree-Sitter:** Designed for modern interactive applications; its incremental parsing model is a boon for IDE integration, though the initial grammar setup can be challenging.
- **Language Workbenches (MPS, Xtext):** Offer an integrated development experience with advanced features, but come with a steeper learning curve and may require commitment to a specific ecosystem.

11.7.2 Performance and Scalability

- **ANTLR and Bison:** Both are highly optimized and suitable for large-scale language processing, though ANTLR's recursive-descent approach might require special handling for left recursion.
- **Lemon:** Excels in low-resource environments due to its lightweight design.
- **PEG-Based Generators:** Provide deterministic parsing with the trade-off of potentially complex grammars; performance is generally good, but highly ambiguous grammars can slow down processing.
- **Parser Combinators:** Often less performant for very large inputs compared to generated parsers, but their modularity allows for optimization at the combinator level.
- **Tree-Sitter:** Excels in scenarios where incremental parsing is required, offering significant performance advantages for interactive applications.

- **Language Workbenches:** Their performance can vary based on the complexity of the DSL and the integration with the host environment; generally, they are optimized for developer productivity rather than raw speed.

11.7.3 Error Reporting and Debugging

- **ANTLR:** Known for its rich error reporting and integrated debugging tools, especially with ANTLRWorks.
- **Bison:** Provides improved error messages over YACC but may still require manual refinement for complex grammars.
- **PEG-Based Tools:** Typically offer clear error messages due to the unambiguous nature of PEGs; however, debugging may involve understanding the ordered choice mechanism.
- **Parser Combinators:** Benefit from the host language's debugging tools, which can lead to very informative error messages, particularly in strongly-typed functional languages.
- **Tree-Sitter:** Designed with modern error handling in mind, it provides incremental updates and rich context, making it ideal for interactive applications.
- **Language Workbenches:** Often include advanced error reporting and correction features, which are integrated into the editor, providing a seamless debugging experience.

11.8 Integration with Modern Development Environments

Modern alternatives are not just about generating efficient parsers; they also integrate closely with contemporary development environments to enhance productivity and usability.

11.8.1 IDE Integration

- **ANTLRWorks and Xtext:** Both provide powerful IDE support. ANTLRWorks offers a visual interface for testing grammars, visualizing parse trees, and debugging. Xtext, integrated with Eclipse, generates full-featured editors with syntax highlighting, auto-completion, and real-time error checking.
- **Tree-Sitter:** Widely used in modern text editors like Atom, Neovim, and VS Code for real-time code analysis, enabling features like syntax highlighting, code folding, and navigation.
- **Language Workbenches:** Tools such as JetBrains MPS allow for projectional editing, which redefines how code is written and maintained, offering a highly interactive and visually oriented development experience.

11.8.2 Continuous Integration and Testing

Modern parser generators often come with built-in support or integrations for automated testing and continuous integration. For example, ANTLR grammars can be integrated into CI pipelines to automatically run regression tests, ensuring that changes to the grammar do not break existing functionality. Similarly, tools like Tree-Sitter can be tested using snapshot tests that compare expected parse trees with actual outputs.

11.8.3 Cross-Platform Support

Many modern alternatives provide cross-platform capabilities, allowing developers to build parsers that run on Windows, macOS, and Linux without significant changes. This is particularly valuable for open-source projects and commercial applications that target multiple operating systems.

11.9 Case Studies: Modern Alternatives in Action

To illustrate the practical benefits of modern alternatives, we present several case studies highlighting real-world applications.

11.9.1 A Modern Language Interpreter with ANTLR

Consider a project that implements an interpreter for a new scripting language. The team chose ANTLR because of its robust error handling, extensive documentation, and multi-language support. The grammar was defined in a single ANTLR file, and the generated parser was integrated into a Java-based interpreter. With the help of ANTLRWorks, the team was able to visualize the parse trees and refine the grammar iteratively. The result was an interpreter that provided meaningful error messages, interactive debugging, and a rapid development cycle. This case study underscores the advantages of using ANTLR for projects that require both high performance and developer-friendly tools.

11.9.2 Building a DSL with Xtext

An enterprise application required a DSL for configuring business workflows. The development team selected Xtext due to its tight integration with the Eclipse IDE and its ability to generate a full-featured editor automatically. Using Xtext, the team defined the grammar of the DSL, and the framework generated an Eclipse-based editor complete with auto-completion and real-time syntax checking. The DSL was then integrated with backend services to process and execute workflows. The project demonstrated that language workbenches like Xtext can significantly reduce development time and improve maintainability for domain-specific languages.

11.9.3 Interactive Code Analysis with Tree-Sitter

In another case, a team developing a modern code editor integrated Tree-Sitter to provide real-time syntax highlighting and code navigation. By leveraging Tree-Sitter's incremental parsing capabilities, the editor was able to update its parse tree as the user typed, without noticeable lag. This enabled advanced features such as error squiggles, code folding, and context-aware navigation, all of which enhanced the overall user experience. The successful deployment of Tree-Sitter in a high-performance, interactive environment highlights its suitability for modern development tools.

11.9.4 Functional Parsing with Parsec

A research group working on a new DSL for data analysis implemented their parser using Haskell's Parsec library. The team appreciated Parsec's modularity and composability, which allowed them to build the parser incrementally and test individual components thoroughly. The resulting parser was not only concise and expressive but also provided excellent error messages that facilitated rapid iteration during development. This case study demonstrates that parser combinators, although requiring a functional programming background, can yield highly maintainable and elegant solutions for complex parsing tasks.

11.10 Future Trends and Emerging Technologies

The landscape of language parsing continues to evolve, and several emerging trends are shaping the future of compiler construction and language processing.

11.10.1 Machine Learning and AI in Parsing

Recent research has explored the application of machine learning to improve parsing technology. For instance, models trained on large code corpora can predict likely parsing errors, suggest corrections, or even automatically generate parts of the grammar. While still in its early stages, the integration of AI into parser generation could lead to more adaptive and resilient systems that learn from usage patterns and evolve over time.

11.10.2 Incremental and Just-In-Time (JIT) Compilation

Tools like Tree-Sitter have already popularized incremental parsing in interactive environments. In parallel, just-in-time (JIT) compilation techniques are being integrated into language processing tools to optimize code at runtime. These approaches blur the lines between compile-time and run-time, offering dynamic optimizations that can adapt to changing workloads. Future parser generators may incorporate JIT techniques to provide real-time performance enhancements.

11.10.3 Domain-Specific Language (DSL) Ecosystems

As businesses increasingly rely on DSLs for specialized tasks, the demand for integrated language workbenches and DSL frameworks is growing. Modern tools like JetBrains MPS and Xtext are continually evolving to support more complex languages, better integration with enterprise systems, and enhanced user interfaces. The future may see even more seamless integration of DSLs into general-purpose programming environments.

11.10.4 Cloud-Based Parsing and Compilation Services

With the advent of cloud computing, there is a growing interest in cloud-based compilers and parsing services. These services can offload intensive parsing and compilation tasks to powerful cloud servers, providing real-time feedback and optimization for distributed development teams. Such solutions can integrate with CI/CD pipelines, offering scalable, on-demand language processing capabilities.

11.10.5 Integration with Modern IDEs and Developer Tools

Modern alternatives are increasingly integrated with state-of-the-art IDEs. Expect to see tighter integration of parser generators with features like real-time error detection, semantic code analysis, and automated refactoring. This trend will further lower the barrier to entry for language development and enhance productivity for both novice and experienced developers.

11.11 Concluding Thoughts

The evolution from FLEX and YACC to modern alternatives represents a significant shift in how we approach language processing. While the foundational ideas remain, the modern tools we've discussed in this chapter offer enhanced error handling, better performance, and deeper integration with contemporary development environments. They open new possibilities for rapid prototyping, interactive development, and the creation of robust, scalable language processing systems.

Modern parser generators, PEG-based tools, parser combinators, and language workbenches each have their unique strengths and are tailored to different use cases. Whether you are building a full-fledged compiler, an interpreter for a DSL, or a real-time code analysis tool, these modern alternatives provide the flexibility and power needed to meet today's software development challenges.

The shift toward more interactive, user-friendly, and adaptable tools reflects the broader trends in software development. As projects grow in complexity and the need for rapid feedback becomes paramount, the limitations of traditional tools like FLEX and YACC become more apparent. Embracing modern alternatives not only improves the technical capabilities of your language processing systems but also enhances the overall developer experience.

Looking to the future, the integration of machine learning, JIT compilation, and cloud-based services will likely redefine what is possible in compiler construction. These trends point to a future where parsers are not only more efficient but also smarter, more adaptive, and more deeply integrated into every stage of the software development lifecycle.